WORLD SERIES 2012

THE YEAR
OF THE

SAN FRANCISCO
GIANTS

CELEBRATING THE 2012 WORLD SERIES® CHAMPIONS

LIBRARY AND ARCHIVES CANADA CATALOGUING IN PUBLICATION

The Year of The San Francisco Giants: Celebrating the 2012 World Series Champions / Major League Baseball.

ISBN 978-0-7710-5729-8

1. World Series (Baseball) (2012).
I. Major League Baseball (Organization)

GV878.4.W674 2012   796.357'646   C2012-901302-1

Published simultaneously in the United States of America by Fenn/McClelland & Stewart, a division of Random House of Canada Limited
P.O. Box 1030, Plattsburgh, New York 12901

Library of Congress Control Number: 2012933530

Printed and bound in the United States of America

Fenn/McClelland & Stewart, a division of Random House of Canada Limited
One Toronto Street
Suite 300
Toronto, Ontario
M5C 2V6
www.randomhouse.com

WORLD SERIES 2012

THE YEAR
OF THE

SAN FRANCISCO
GIANTS

CELEBRATING THE 2012 WORLD SERIES® CHAMPIONS

FENN
M&S

CONTENTS

EVEN THOUGH THEY had a better regular-season record than their opponent, the San Francisco Giants seemed like resilient underdogs heading into the 2012 Fall Classic against the Detroit Tigers. Coming back from the brink of elimination in both the Division Series and the League Championship Series had earned the team a never-say-die epithet that belied a deep rotation, a well-balanced lineup and a World Series trophy only two years old. Meanwhile, the Motor City was home to arguably the best pitcher and the best hitter during the 162-game marathon from April to October. But both came up short under the bright lights of baseball's biggest stage and left room for new heroes to emerge in orange and black.

From undeniable ace Matt Cain; to accomplished 23-year-old Madison Bumgarner; to journeyman — all the way to Japan and back — Ryan Vogelsong; to the resurgent Barry Zito; to two-time Cy Young Award winner Tim Lincecum excelling in a new role; to eccentric closer Sergio Romo filling in for the even more eccentric Brian Wilson, the Giants' pitching staff limited Detroit's powerful bats to a mere six runs over four games. The offense got an early boost from a historic three-homer performance from Series MVP Pablo Sandoval on the opening night of the Fall Classic. The Panda stayed strong for the rest of the Series and was joined on the offensive by NL batting champion and team leader Buster Posey, as well as new additions this year in Angel Pagan, Gregor Blanco and NLCS MVP Marco Scutaro.

Under the guidance of Bruce Bochy, a group of talented players became an unstoppable team. "It's amazing what a club can do when it plays as a team and is unselfish and does whatever it can to help win. That's what these guys did," Bochy, now the proud owner of two Commissioner's Trophies, said of his 2012 Giants. Midseason acquisition Hunter Pence became a leader in the clubhouse for his ability to inspire that team spirit with his impassioned speeches and the ritual pregame "slow clap" — with an accompanying chant that started out subdued and grew into a boisterous force. It is a fitting metaphor for the team that fell behind early in the postseason only to win seven straight games to cap an incredible run with a sweep of the Tigers.

Capturing it all — every pitch, every swing, every momentous hit and defensive play — were MLB editors and photographers, preserving the 2012 Fall Classic in stories and images that will be forever emblazoned in the memories of those who witnessed the Series, who relished every out and every dramatic turn of events. This year's Fall Classic was another reminder of the joy that comes with watching baseball, and although no single quote or image could ever truly capture the breadth of emotion felt by players and fans during those moments, the stories they do tell serve as a reminder of a landmark event.

ASSEMBLING THE PIECES

AFTER A WORLD SERIES win in 2010, it made sense to keep the Giants' core, such as Buster Posey and Matt Cain, intact. But a second-place finish in '11 encouraged General Manager Brian Sabean to make a few key additions, including Angel Pagan, Marco Scutaro and Hunter Pence, that paid off in a big way as the Giants soared to their second title in three years.

Draft

Brandon Belt — 5th round, 2009

Madison Bumgarner — 1st round, 2007

Emmanuel Burriss — Compensatory, 2006

Matt Cain — 1st round, 2002

Brandon Crawford — 4th round, 2008

Tim Lincecum — 1st round, 2006

Brett Pill — 7th round, 2006

Buster Posey — 1st round, 2008

Sergio Romo — 28th round, 2005

Brian Wilson — 24th round, 2003

Free Agency

Jeremy Affeldt — 3 years/$14M (2008)

Joaquin Arias — Pre-arbitration eligible (2011)

Gregor Blanco — 1 year/$516K (2011)

Santiago Casilla — 1 year/$1.3.M, second-year arbitration eligible (2010)

Clay Hensley — 1 year/$750K, arbitration eligible (2012)

Aubrey Huff — 2 years/$22M, plus option (2010)

Jose Mijares — 1 year/$925K, first-year arbitration eligible (2012)

Guillermo Mota — 1 year/$1M (2011)

Xavier Nady — 1 year/$700K (2012)

Brad Penny — 1 year/$480K (2012)

Hector Sanchez — 1 year/$480K (2006)

Pablo Sandoval — 3 years/$17.15M (2003)

Ryan Theriot — 1 year/$1.25M, third-year arbitration eligible (2012)

Ryan Vogelsong — 2 years/$8.3M, 2014 team option (2011)

Barry Zito — 7 years/$126M, 2014 team option (2006)

Trade

George Kontos — from NYY for Chris Stewart (2012)

Javier Lopez — from PIT for Joe Martinez and John Bowker (2010)

Angel Pagan — from NYM for Ramon Ramirez and Andres Torres (2011)

Hunter Pence — from PHI for Seth Rosin, Tommy Joseph and Nate Schierholtz (2012)

Marco Scutaro — from COL with cash for Charlie Culberson (2012)

Date	Opp.	Res.	R	RA	W-L	Date	Opp.	Res.	R	RA	W-L
Friday, April 6	@ ARI	L	4	5	0-1	Tuesday, May 22	@ MIL	W	6	4	23-20
Saturday, April 7	@ ARI	L	4	5	0-2	Wednesday, May 23	@ MIL	L	5	8	23-21
Sunday, April 8	@ ARI	L	6	7	0-3	Thursday, May 24	@ MIA	W	14	7	24-21
Monday, April 9	@ COL	W	7	0	1-3	Friday, May 25	@ MIA	L	6	7	24-22
Wednesday, April 11	@ COL	L	8	17	1-4	Saturday, May 26	@ MIA	L	3	5	24-23
Thursday, April 12	@ COL	W	4	2	2-4	Sunday, May 27	@ MIA	W	3	2	25-23
Friday, April 13	PIT	W	5	0	3-4	Monday, May 28	ARI	W	4	2	26-23
Saturday, April 14	PIT	W	4	3	4-4	Tuesday, May 29	ARI	W	3	1	27-23
Sunday, April 15	PIT	L	1	4	4-5	Wednesday, May 30	ARI	L	1	4	27-24
Monday, April 16	PHI	L	2	5	4-6	Friday, June 1	CHC	W	4	3	28-24
Tuesday, April 17	PHI	W	4	2	5-6	Saturday, June 2	CHC	W	2	1	29-24
Wednesday, April 18	PHI	W	1	0	6-6	Sunday, June 3	CHC	W	2	0	30-24
Friday, April 20	@ NYM	W	4	3	7-6	Monday, June 4	CHC	W	3	2	31-24
Saturday, April 21	@ NYM	L	4	5	7-7	Tuesday, June 5	@ SD	L	5	6	31-25
Monday, April 23	@ NYM	W	6	1	8-7	Wednesday, June 6	@ SD	W	6	5	32-25
Monday, April 23	@ NYM	W	7	2	9-7	Thursday, June 7	@ SD	W	8	3	33-25
Tuesday, April 24	@ CIN	L	2	9	9-8	Friday, June 8	TEX	L	0	5	33-26
Wednesday, April 25	@ CIN	L	2	4	9-9	Saturday, June 9	TEX	W	5	2	34-26
Thursday, April 26	@ CIN	W	6	5	10-9	Sunday, June 10	TEX	L	0	5	34-27
Friday, April 27	SD	L	3	5	10-10	Tuesday, June 12	HOU	W	6	3	35-27
Saturday, April 28	SD	W	2	1	11-10	Wednesday, June 13	HOU	W	10	0	36-27
Sunday, April 29	SD	W	4	1	12-10	Thursday, June 14	HOU	L	3	6	36-28
Tuesday, May 1	MIA	L	1	2	12-11	Friday, June 15	@ SEA	W	4	2	37-28
Wednesday, May 2	MIA	L	2	3	12-12	Saturday, June 16	@ SEA	L	4	7	37-29
Thursday, May 3	MIA	L	2	3	12-13	Sunday, June 17	@ SEA	L	1	2	37-30
Friday, May 4	MIL	L	4	6	12-14	Monday, June 18	@ LAA	W	5	3	38-30
Saturday, May 5	MIL	W	5	2	13-14	Tuesday, June 19	@ LAA	L	5	12	38-31
Sunday, May 6	MIL	W	4	3	14-14	Wednesday, June 20	@ LAA	L	0	6	38-32
Monday, May 7	@ LAD	L	1	9	14-15	Friday, June 22	@ OAK	W	5	4	39-32
Tuesday, May 8	@ LAD	W	2	1	15-15	Saturday, June 23	@ OAK	W	9	8	40-32
Wednesday, May 9	@ LAD	L	2	6	15-16	Sunday, June 24	@ OAK	L	2	4	40-33
Friday, May 11	@ ARI	L	1	5	15-17	Monday, June 25	LAD	W	8	0	41-33
Saturday, May 12	@ ARI	W	5	2	16-17	Tuesday, June 26	LAD	W	2	0	42-33
Sunday, May 13	@ ARI	W	7	3	17-17	Wednesday, June 27	LAD	W	3	0	43-33
Monday, May 14	COL	W	3	2	18-17	Thursday, June 28	CIN	W	5	0	44-33
Tuesday, May 15	COL	L	4	5	18-18	Friday, June 29	CIN	L	1	5	44-34
Wednesday, May 16	STL	L	1	4	18-19	Saturday, June 30	CIN	L	1	2	44-35
Thursday, May 17	STL	W	7	5	19-19	Sunday, July 1	CIN	W	4	3	45-35
Friday, May 18	OAK	W	8	6	20-19	Tuesday, July 3	@ WAS	L	3	9	45-36
Saturday, May 19	OAK	W	4	0	21-19	Wednesday, July 4	@ WAS	L	4	9	45-37
Sunday, May 20	OAK	L	2	6	21-20	Thursday, July 5	@ WAS	L	5	6	45-38
Monday, May 21	@MIL	W	4	3	22-20	Friday, July 6	@ PIT	W	6	5	46-38

REGULAR-SEASON RESULTS

Date	Opp.	Res.	R	RA	W-L	Date	Opp.	Res.	R	RA	W-L
Saturday, July 7	@ PIT	L	1	3	46-39	Saturday, Aug. 25	ATL	L	3	7	71-56
Sunday, July 8	@ PIT	L	2	13	46-40	Sunday, Aug. 26	ATL	L	1	7	71-57
Friday, July 13	HOU	W	5	1	47-40	Tuesday, Aug. 28	@ HOU	W	3	2	72-57
Saturday, July 14	HOU	W	3	2	48-40	Wednesday, Aug. 29	@ HOU	W	6	4	73-57
Sunday, July 15	HOU	W	3	2	49-40	Thursday, Aug. 30	@ HOU	W	8	4	74-57
Tuesday, July 17	@ ATL	W	9	0	50-40	Friday, Aug. 31	@ CHC	L	4	6	74-58
Wednesday, July 18	@ ATL	W	9	4	51-40	Saturday, Sept. 1	@ CHC	W	5	2	75-58
Thursday, July 19	@ ATL	L	2	3	51-41	Sunday, Sept. 2	@ CHC	W	7	5	76-58
Friday, July 20	@ PHI	W	7	2	52-41	Monday, Sept. 3	ARI	W	9	8	77-58
Saturday, July 21	@ PHI	W	6	5	53-41	Tuesday, Sept. 4	ARI	L	6	8	77-59
Sunday, July 22	@ PHI	L	3	4	53-42	Wednesday, Sept. 5	ARI	L	2	6	77-60
Monday, July 23	SD	W	7	1	54-42	Friday, Sept. 7	LAD	W	5	2	78-60
Tuesday, July 24	SD	W	3	2	55-42	Saturday, Sept. 8	LAD	L	2	3	78-61
Wednesday, July 25	SD	L	3	6	55-43	Sunday, Sept. 9	LAD	W	4	0	79-61
Friday, July 27	LAD	L	3	5	55-44	Monday, Sept. 10	@ COL	L	5	6	79-62
Saturday, July 28	LAD	L	0	10	55-45	Tuesday, Sept. 11	@ COL	W	9	8	80-62
Sunday, July 29	LAD	L	0	4	55-46	Wednesday, Sept. 12	@ COL	W	8	3	81-62
Monday, July 30	NYM	L	7	8	55-47	Friday, Sept. 14	@ ARI	W	6	2	82-62
Tuesday, July 31	NYM	W	4	1	56-47	Saturday, Sept. 15	@ ARI	W	3	2	83-62
Wednesday, Aug. 1	NYM	L	1	2	56-48	Sunday, Sept. 16	@ ARI	L	2	10	83-63
Thursday, Aug. 2	NYM	L	1	9	56-49	Monday, Sept. 17	COL	W	2	1	84-63
Friday, Aug. 3	@ COL	W	16	4	57-49	Tuesday, Sept. 18	COL	W	6	3	85-63
Saturday, Aug. 4	@ COL	W	11	6	58-49	Wednesday, Sept. 19	COL	W	7	1	86-63
Sunday, Aug. 5	@ COL	W	8	3	59-49	Thursday, Sept. 20	COL	W	9	2	87-63
Monday, Aug. 6	@ STL	L	2	8	59-50	Friday, Sept. 21	SD	W	5	1	88-63
Tuesday, Aug. 7	@ STL	W	4	2	60-50	Saturday, Sept. 22	SD	W	8	4	89-63
Wednesday, Aug. 8	@ STL	W	15	0	61-50	Sunday, Sept. 23	SD	L	4	6	89-64
Thursday, Aug. 9	@ STL	L	1	3	61-51	Tuesday, Sept. 25	ARI	L	2	7	89-65
Friday, Aug. 10	COL	L	0	3	61-52	Wednesday, Sept. 26	ARI	W	6	0	90-65
Saturday, Aug. 11	COL	W	9	3	62-52	Thursday, Sept. 27	ARI	W	7	3	91-65
Sunday, Aug. 12	COL	W	9	6	63-52	Friday, Sept. 28	@ SD	W	3	1	92-65
Monday, Aug. 13	WAS	L	2	14	63-53	Saturday, Sept. 29	@ SD	L	3	7	92-66
Tuesday, Aug. 14	WAS	W	6	1	64-53	Sunday, Sept. 30	@ SD	W	7	5	93-66
Wednesday, Aug. 15	WAS	L	4	6	64-54	Monday, Oct. 1	@ LAD	L	2	3	93-67
Friday, Aug. 17	@ SD	W	10	1	65-54	Tuesday, Oct. 2	@ LAD	W	4	3	94-67
Saturday, Aug. 18	@ SD	W	8	7	66-54	Wednesday, Oct. 3	@ LAD	L	1	5	94-68
Sunday, Aug. 19	@ SD	L	1	7	66-55						
Monday, Aug. 20	@ LAD	W	2	1	67-55						
Tuesday, Aug. 21	@ LAD	W	4	1	68-55						
Wednesday, Aug. 22	@ LAD	W	8	4	69-55						
Thursday, Aug. 23	ATL	W	5	2	70-55						
Friday, Aug. 24	ATL	W	5	3	71-55						

NO.	PLAYER	B/T	W	L	ERA	SO	BB	SV	BIRTHDATE	BIRTHPLACE
PITCHERS										
41	Jeremy Affeldt	L/L	1	2	2.70	57	23	3	6/6/79	Phoenix, AZ
40	Madison Bumgarner	R/L	16	11	3.37	191	49	0	8/1/89	Hickory, NC
18	Matt Cain	R/R	16	5	2.79	193	51	0	10/1/84	Dothan, AL
46	Santiago Casilla	R/R	7	6	2.84	55	22	25	7/25/80	San Cristobal, D.R.
70	George Kontos	R/R	2	1	2.47	44	12	0	6/12/85	Lincolnwood, IL
55	Tim Lincecum	L/R	10	15	5.18	190	90	0	6/15/84	Bellevue, WA
49	Javier Lopez	L/L	3	0	2.50	28	14	7	7/11/77	San Juan, P.R.
50	Jose Mijares	L/L	1	0	2.55	20	8	0	10/29/84	Caracas, Venezuela
59	Guillermo Mota	R/R	0	1	5.23	24	8	0	7/25/73	San Pedro de Macoris, D.R.
54	Sergio Romo	R/R	4	2	1.79	63	10	14	3/4/83	Brawley, CA
32	Ryan Vogelsong	R/R	14	9	3.37	158	62	0	7/22/77	Charlotte, NC
75	Barry Zito	L/L	15	8	4.15	114	70	0	5/13/78	Las Vegas, NV

NO.	PLAYER	B/T	AB	H	AVG	HR	RBI	OBP	BIRTHDATE	BIRTHPLACE
CATCHERS										
28	Buster Posey	R/R	530	178	.336	24	103	.408	3/27/87	Leesburg, GA
29	Hector Sanchez	S/R	218	61	.280	3	34	.295	11/17/89	Maracay, Venezuela
INFIELDERS										
13	Joaquin Arias	R/R	319	86	.270	5	34	.304	9/21/84	Santo Domingo, D.R.
9	Brandon Belt	L/L	411	113	.275	7	56	.360	4/20/88	Nacogdoches, TX
35	Brandon Crawford	L/R	435	108	.248	4	45	.304	1/21/87	Mountain View, CA
17	Aubrey Huff	L/R	78	15	.192	1	7	.326	12/20/76	Marion, OH
48	Pablo Sandoval	S/R	396	112	.283	12	63	.342	8/11/86	Puerto Cabello, Venezuela
19	Marco Scutaro	R/R	243	88	.362	3	44	.385	10/30/75	San Felipe, Venezuela
5	Ryan Theriot	R/R	352	95	.270	0	28	.316	12/7/79	Baton Rouge, LA
OUTFIELDERS										
7	Gregor Blanco	L/L	393	96	.244	5	34	.333	12/24/83	Caracas, Venezuela
12	Xavier Nady	R/R	50	12	.240	1	7	.333	11/14/78	Carmel, CA
16	Angel Pagan	S/R	605	174	.288	8	56	.338	7/2/81	Rio Piedras, Puerto Rico
8	Hunter Pence	R/R	219	48	.219	7	45	.287	4/13/83	Fort Worth, TX

Manager: Bruce Bochy (15). Coaches: Tim Flannery (1), Mark Gardner (26), Roberto Kelly (39), Hensley Meulens (37), Dave Righetti (33), Ron Wotus (23).

GAME 1, OCT. 6
REDS 5, GIANTS 2

THE REDS COULD have folded when ace Johnny Cueto was forced to leave the game due to back spasms after facing only one batter, but Cincinnati's stellar makeshift pitching and dynamic bats had other ideas.

Mat Latos was called on for emergency middle relief in the third inning and the usual starter delivered. The 6-foot-6 right-hander threw four innings, allowing just four hits and one run on a homer off the bat of Buster Posey. The only other run the Giants could eke out against the Reds' lockdown pitching was scored on a wild pitch by closer Aroldis Chapman. But against ace right-hander Matt Cain, the Reds' offense had already put the game out of reach. A pair of homers — by Brandon Phillips and Jay Bruce in the third and fourth innings, respectively — gave the Reds an early 3-0 lead.

And Phillips wasn't done, manufacturing an insurance run in the ninth with an RBI single, solidifying the 5-2 opening-game victory.

	1	2	3	4	5	6	7	8	9	R	H	E
CINCINNATI	0	0	2	1	0	0	0	0	2	5	9	1
SAN FRANCISCO	0	0	0	0	0	1	0	0	1	2	7	0

WP: LeCure LP: Cain
HR: CIN: Phillips, Bruce; SF: Posey

Posey smashed a solo shot in the sixth inning — the only run his team mustered against the sharp pitching of Latos out of the bullpen.

Giants infielder Joaquin Arias (left), who entered the game as a pinch-hitter, slid in safely for a run in the ninth inning after Chapman's wild pitch.

"YOU HATE TO SEE ANYBODY LOSE THEIR STARTER, BUT THEY BROUGHT IN A GOOD ONE. LATOS IS TOUGH, AND WE HAD STARTERS THAT COULD GO TONIGHT, TOO. HE WAS AVAILABLE AND CAME IN AND DID A GREAT JOB AGAINST US." Bruce Bochy on Mat Latos filling in for the injured Johnny Cueto

GAME 2, OCT. 7
REDS 9, GIANTS 0

IT'S HARD TO tell which was the more impressive performance in the Reds' 9-0 victory: Bronson Arroyo's masterful seven innings of one-hit, shutout ball, or the potency of the Reds' lineup against a typically effective Giants pitching staff.

Arroyo certainly spearheaded the effort, holding San Francisco hitless until the fifth inning and allowing just two base runners over his whole outing. J.J. Hoover and Jose Arredondo finished what Arroyo started, giving up just one hit combined in their two innings of relief work.

The Reds, meanwhile, out hit the Giants, 13-2, and erupted for nine runs off San Francisco pitching. It was an especially good night to be named Ryan, as Ryans Ludwick and Hanigan combined to go 4 for 7 with one home run and four RBI.

Almost the entire Reds lineup got in on the action in a five-run eighth inning that all but ensured that they would be Ohio-bound with the series firmly in their control.

	1	2	3	4	5	6	7	8	9	R	H	E
CINCINNATI	0	1	0	3	0	0	0	5	0	9	13	0
SAN FRANCISCO	0	0	0	0	0	0	0	0	0	0	2	0

WP: Arroyo LP: Bumgarner
HR: CIN: Ludwick

Lincecum provided a bright spot in the 9-0 defeat, hurling two shutout innings out of the bullpen to prove that he could contribute in his new role.

For the second straight game, Pablo Sandoval and the rest of the San Francisco lineup couldn't crack the Reds' pitching staff, managing just two hits.

"WE KNOW WHERE WE'RE AT RIGHT NOW — OUR BACKS ARE TO THE WALL. WE HAVE TO COME OUT AND BE READY TO PLAY ONCE WE GET TO CINCINNATI. THEY KNOW WHAT'S AT STAKE, AND AS I SAID YESTERDAY, THEY'VE DONE A GREAT JOB ALL YEAR OF BOUNCING BACK. IT'S BEEN DONE BEFORE AND WE HAVE TO KEEP FIGHTING. THERE IS NO CHOICE IN THIS. WE HAVE TO KEEP OUR HEADS UP AND BE READY TO GO COME TUESDAY." Bruce Bochy

GAME 3, OCT. 9
GIANTS 2, REDS 1

FOR THE SECOND straight game, a Reds starter took a no-hitter into the fifth, but in Homer Bailey's 10-strikeout effort, the defense behind him could not hold up.

Down 1-0 in the third, the Giants eked out a run after Gregor Blanco, who reached after being hit by a pitch, scored on a sacrifice fly. The game would remain tied through nine innings thanks to shutdown pitching from both teams, an especially welcome sight from a Giants staff that had allowed 14 runs and 22 hits through the series' first two games.

In the 10th, the dormant Giants' bats awoke, with two straight singles from Buster Posey and Hunter Pence. The next two batters struck out and disappointment loomed again. But after both base runners advanced on a passed ball, Posey scored the go-ahead run after Joaquin Arias reached base on a rare error by Scott Rolen.

Sergio Romo pitched a 1-2-3 10th and kept the series alive for the Giants with a 2-1 win.

	1	2	3	4	5	6	7	8	9	10	R	H	E
SAN FRANCISCO	0	0	1	0	0	0	0	0	0	1	2	3	0
CINCINNATI	1	0	0	0	0	0	0	0	0	0	1	4	1

WP: Romo LP: Broxton

Posey dropped a single into right field to jump-start the Giants' rally in the 10th inning off Jonathan Broxton, eventually scoring on a Rolen error.

"WE DIDN'T DO ANYTHING AGAINST HOMER BAILEY, SO YOU HOPE YOUR PITCHING STAFF COMES THROUGH. AND WHAT A JOB THEY DID: THREE SOLID INNINGS FROM CASILLA, LOPEZ AND ROMO. WHEN YOU'RE IN A GAME LIKE THIS, THAT'S WHAT YOU HOPE FOR." Bruce Bochy

With his team facing elimination, Romo kept hope alive by retiring all six batters he faced in just his second two-inning appearance all season.

GAME 4, OCT. 10
GIANTS 8, REDS 3

THE GIANTS DIDN'T need extra innings or a stroke of luck to win Game 4, just a revitalized offense that put up eight runs and a return to form by Tim Lincecum, who got the win with 4.1 innings of six-strikeout, two-hit relief.

Despite being relegated to the bullpen, Lincecum looked less like the pitcher who struggled in the regular season and more like the one who won back-to-back Cy Young Awards in 2008 and '09. Barry Zito started the contest, but it was Lincecum's stellar outing that helped San Francisco see another day.

He received a critical boost from the Giants' offensive awakening. Angel Pagan set the tone early, connecting on the second pitch of the game for a leadoff home run. Reds spot starter Mike Leake gave up four more runs through 4.1 innings, and after a two-run home run from both Gregor Blanco and Pablo Sandoval, the Giants had erased their two-game deficit to force a winner-take-all play-in for the NLCS.

	1	2	3	4	5	6	7	8	9	R	H	E
SAN FRANCISCO	1	2	0	0	2	0	3	0	0	8	11	1
CINCINNATI	1	0	1	0	0	1	0	0	0	3	9	0

WP: Lincecum LP: Leake
HR: CIN: Ludwick; SF: Pagan, Blanco, Sandoval

Lincecum gave up just two hits and struck out six in 4.1 innings of relief.

Pagan gave his team a much-needed jolt with a leadoff homer on the road.

After hitting just five regular-season homers, Blanco picked a prime time to find his power stroke, slugging a two-run shot in the second.

"RIGHT NOW, I FEEL LIKE THE TIMES ARE DIFFERENT. WE'RE PLAYING FOR A DIFFERENT REASON THAN JUST THE SEASON, TO GET TO THE NLCS AND FURTHER, SO I FEEL WITH THAT MOTIVATION, IT HELPS TO GO INTO THOSE SITUATIONS AND NOT THINK ABOUT THE DIFFERENCE OF STARTING AND BEING IN A BULLPEN SITUATION. I'VE JUST GOT TO GET MY OUTS AND DO MY JOB." Tim Lincecum

GAME 5, OCT. 11
GIANTS 6, REDS 4

IN NLDS HISTORY, no team had ever come back to win a best-of-five series after losing its first two games, let alone win three straight on the road in order to do so. With a 6-4 Game 5 victory, the Giants became the first.

The rubber match remained scoreless through four, with Matt Cain and Mat Latos working around sporadic hits. But a six-run fifth inning saw the away team break the game wide open, highlighted by an emphatic grand slam off the bat of Buster Posey.

From there, all the Giants had to do was hold on, although the Reds would not make it easy. Cincinnati had at least two runners on in each of the last three innings, but the San Francisco bullpen never allowed that clutch, game-changing hit.

Sergio Romo worked out of a jam in the ninth as the Giants completed their unprecedented comeback and punched their ticket to the NLCS.

	1	2	3	4	5	6	7	8	9	R	H	E
SAN FRANCISCO	0	0	0	0	6	0	0	0	0	6	9	1
CINCINNATI	0	0	0	0	2	1	0	0	1	4	12	1

WP: Cain LP: Latos SV: Romo
HR: CIN: Ludwick; SF: Posey

Posey capped a six-run, fifth-inning rally by crushing a grand slam to left field — a blow that proved to be the signature moment of the Giants' comeback.

Cain gutted out 5.2 innings without his best stuff, allowing a two-run double in the fifth but ultimately notching his third career postseason victory.

GAME 5, OCT. 11
GIANTS 6, REDS 4

Romo (right) and Posey congratulated each other after the closer struck out Scott Rolen to end Game 5 and secure his first playoff save.

"WE HAVE A UNIQUE CHEMISTRY. IT'S DEFINITELY HARD TO EXPLAIN IN WORDS, BUT YOU CAN JUST FEEL EVERYONE REALLY COMING TO-GETHER, EVERYONE PLAYING FOR EACH OTHER." Hunter Pence

The Giants celebrated on the field in Cincinnati after becoming the first NL team ever to overcome a 2-games-to-none Division Series deficit.

GAME 1, OCT. 14
CARDINALS 6, GIANTS 4

IN THE FINAL game of the Division Series, the Cardinals found themselves on the wrong side of a 6-0 score by the end of the third inning. They eventually overcame the deficit — and then some — to advance. But in the first game of the NLCS, they proved that it's nice to not have to rely on late-inning heroics by posting their own six-run lead early in the game against the Giants.

Last postseason's hometown hero, David Freese, kicked off the scoring in the second with a two-run home run. The Redbirds tacked on four more in the fourth through timely hitting and Carlos Beltran's 14th career postseason homer.

The Giants manufactured four runs of their own in the bottom of the frame with four consecutive clutch, two-out hits. But after that, it was lights out as both teams turned to their stellar bullpens, leaving the score at 6-4 in favor of St. Louis at the end of the game.

	1	2	3	4	5	6	7	8	9	R	H	E
ST. LOUIS	0	2	0	4	0	0	0	0	0	6	8	0
SAN FRANCISCO	0	0	0	4	0	0	0	0	0	4	7	1

WP: Mujica **LP:** Bumgarner **SV:** Motte
HR: STL: Beltran, Freese

Brandon Belt hit a two-out RBI single as part of a four-run fourth, but the team fell short of overtaking the Cardinals in Game 1 of the NLCS.

Freese slugged his only home run of the 2012 postseason in the second inning of Game 1 to put the Cardinals on the board first. Edward Mujica earned the win for St. Louis, pitching a perfect seventh and striking out the side.

"THE GUYS DID A GREAT JOB OF BATTLING BACK. THE BULLPEN DID A GREAT JOB. ST. LOUIS GOT A BREAK HERE OR THERE AND MADE A GREAT PLAY ON PAGAN'S BALL UP THE MIDDLE. IT WAS A HARD-FOUGHT GAME." Bruce Bochy

GAME 2, OCT. 15
GIANTS 7, CARDINALS 1

THE GIANTS WERE eager to even the ledger in Game 2, jumping out to an early lead with a solo homer by leadoff man Angel Pagan. Chris Carpenter was not the postseason powerhouse he had been in previous starts — although he helped himself with an RBI double in the top of the second — and was pulled after giving up five runs in four innings. Carpenter's RBI was all the offense St. Louis would muster. After the Giants had leaned heavily on their bullpen to that point in the postseason, Ryan Vogelsong became their first starter to go more than six innings, tossing seven frames and only allowing one run.

A hard slide by Matt Holliday in the top of the first eventually sent second baseman Marco Scutaro to the hospital to get X-rays on his leg, but not before he exacted revenge with a three-run, bases-loaded single that gave San Francisco a four-run lead. Ryan Theriot, who came in to replace Scutaro, knocked in two more with a base hit of his own in the eighth to put the final score at 7-1.

	1	2	3	4	5	6	7	8	9	R	H	E
ST. LOUIS	0	1	0	0	0	0	0	0	0	1	5	2
SAN FRANCISCO	1	0	0	4	0	0	0	2	x	7	12	0

WP: Vogelsong LP: C. Carpenter
HR: SF: Pagan

As part of an explosive Giants offense in Game 2, Theriot muscled an RBI single in the eighth to put the game out of reach.

Vogelsong has enjoyed a resurgence since returning last year to the team that drafted him, pitching seven quality frames in the Giants' first NLCS win.

"I JUST REALLY TRIED TO KEEP MIXING IT UP. DEPENDING ON THE HITTER AND THE SITUATION, I TRIED TO BOUNCE THE BALL AROUND THE ZONE LIKE I NORMALLY DO."
Ryan Vogelsong

GAME 2, OCT. 15
GIANTS 7, CARDINALS 1

A hard slide by Holliday sent Scutaro to the ground and later out of the game, but not before he gave the Giants the lead with a two-run single.

Despite taking the loss, Carpenter knocked in the Cardinals' only run of the game on a double.

COMING INTO HIS OWN

A PRODUCT OF the small Kutztown University in his native Pennsylvania, Ryan Vogelsong got off to a slow start in his pursuit of the Big Leagues. He was drafted by the Giants in the fifth round of the 1998 Draft and made his MLB debut in September just two years later. But from there, the tall righty struggled to find consistency and control. He bounced between the starting rotation and the bullpen in Pittsburgh, spent three years in Japan and was released from Minor League contracts with both the Phillies and the Angels before re-signing with the Giants in 2011. His strong starts in place of the injured Barry Zito earned him a spot on the All-Star roster that year. This season, he topped even that breakout performance, leading the league with a 2.36 ERA at the All-Star break and limiting the Cardinals to two runs over 14 innings in the NLCS.

GAME 3, OCT. 17
CARDINALS 3, GIANTS 1

WHEN SEVEN-TIME All-Star Carlos Beltran strained his left knee in the first inning and had to exit the game, it was reasonable to think that the Cardinals' offense would suffer in his absence. But in his first at-bat, Beltran's replacement, Matt Carpenter, smashed a two-run blast off Giants ace Matt Cain, quickly negating the one run that San Francisco had scored in the top of the frame.

The Giants, on the other hand, were unable to capitalize on St. Louis starter Kyle Lohse's mistakes, plating just one of the 12 base runners that he allowed through the first 5.2 innings. The Cardinals tacked on another run on a groundout in the seventh to put the score at 3-1 in their favor. And that is exactly where it stayed a 208-minute rain delay and two innings later, after Jason Motte converted the first six-out save of his career to give St. Louis a 2-games-to-1 advantage in the series.

	1	2	3	4	5	6	7	8	9	R	H	E
SAN FRANCISCO	0	0	1	0	0	0	0	0	0	1	9	1
ST. LOUIS	0	0	2	0	0	0	1	0	x	3	6	0

WP: Lohse LP: Cain S: Motte
HR: STL: M. Carpenter

This year's All-Star Game winner and the Giants' No. 1 starter, Cain took the loss in Game 4 after giving up three runs in 6.2 innings.

Carpenter (above) did a stellar job filling Beltran's shoes after the slugger left the game with knee trouble, securing a lead for the Cardinals with his two-run shot in the third. A torrential downpour delayed play for more than three hours at Busch Stadium.

"I TRY TO FIGHT WHEN I'M UP THERE AND GRIND OUT THOSE AT-BATS. TODAY WAS AN EXAMPLE OF THAT. I WAS AT 0-2 AND WORKED MY WAY BACK TO A 2-2 COUNT, WHEN HE THREW A SLIDER AND I WAS ABLE TO PUT A GOOD SWING ON IT."
Matt Carpenter

GAME 4, OCT. 18
CARDINALS 8, GIANTS 3

THE GIANTS HOPED that the nearly flawless relief work from Tim Lincecum to that point in the postseason was a sign that the two-time Cy Young Award winner was past his uncharacteristically rough regular season. But before he could get out of the first inning in his Game 4 start, the four-time All-Star had given up two runs to a determined Cardinals offense.

Hunter Pence halved the lead in the top of the second with a homer to snap his NLCS slump and Lincecum bounced back to retire eight batters in a row. But the Cardinals chased him from the game in the fifth and the Giants' bullpen fared no better, eventually allowing four more runs in the 8-3 loss. Adam Wainwright pitched seven innings of four-hit ball to earn his first win of the playoffs and bring St. Louis within one game of advancing to the World Series.

	1	2	3	4	5	6	7	8	9	R	H	E
SAN FRANCISCO	0	1	0	0	0	0	0	0	2	3	6	1
ST. LOUIS	2	0	0	0	2	2	2	0	x	8	12	0

WP: Wainwright LP: Lincecum
HR: SF: Pence, Sandoval

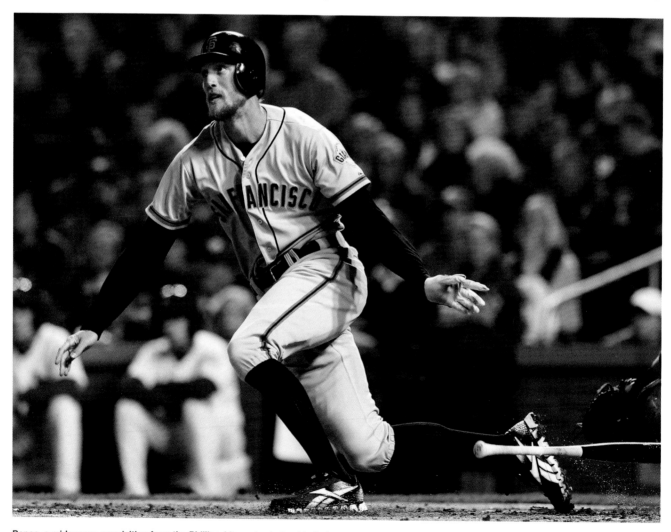

Pence, a midseason acquisition from the Phillies, hit a solo shot — his first career postseason longball — in the second inning of the Game 4 loss.

"A PART OF ME WANTED TO PROVE TO MYSELF THAT I COULD GO OUT THERE AND PITCH GREAT WHEN WE NEEDED ME TO. I WAS VERY CONFIDENT IN MY ABILITY AND MY STUFF. I JUST NEEDED TO TRUST IT AND GO OUT THERE AND MAKE PITCHES, AND TONIGHT I WAS ABLE TO EXECUTE."
Adam Wainwright

Wainwright kept the Giants' bats quiet after Pence's home run, earning the win for his seven innings of one-run ball.

GAME 5, OCT. 19
GIANTS 5, CARDINALS 0

IT HAS BEEN 10 years since Barry Zito won the AL Cy Young Award with the Oakland A's. The decade since has not always been kind to the southpaw, who was left off the Giants' postseason roster in 2010. But facing a win-or-go-home situation in St. Louis, Zito looked like his old self out on the mound in Game 5. He pitched 7.2 shutout innings, striking out six and retiring 11 straight at one point.

He even contributed offensively during a four-run fourth inning. A throwing error by opposing pitcher Lance Lynn on Hunter Pence's dribbler up the middle allowed the first run to score after singles by Marco Scutaro and Pablo Sandoval. Brandon Crawford's two-run single kept the inning alive and set up an RBI bunt single for Zito. Sandoval's solo home run in the eighth secured the Giants' 5-0 win and their trip back to San Francisco to close out the series.

	1	2	3	4	5	6	7	8	9	R	H	E
SAN FRANCISCO	0	0	0	4	0	0	0	1	0	5	6	0
ST. LOUIS	0	0	0	0	0	0	0	0	0	0	7	1

WP: Zito LP: Lynn
HR: SF: Sandoval

After a four-run fourth gave the Giants a comfortable lead, Kung Fu Panda smacked a solo shot in the eighth for good measure.

With Brian Wilson on the DL all season, Sergio Romo became the Giants' postseason closer and filled in admirably, securing the do-or-die Game 5 win.

"I COULDN'T BE HAPPIER FOR ZITO. I DON'T KNOW HOW MANY TIMES WHEN WE NEEDED TO WIN THIS YEAR, HE FOUND A WAY TO GET IT DONE FOR US — ALTHOUGH NOT QUITE THE SAME GAME THAT HE PITCHED TONIGHT WITH WHAT WAS AT STAKE. BUT WE'VE WON 13 STRAIGHT WITH HIM ON THE MOUND NOW." Bruce Bochy

GAME 5, OCT. 19
GIANTS 5, CARDINALS 0

RALLY ZITO

COMING INTO GAME 5 of the NLCS, the Cardinals had momentum after winning the previous game, they had home-field advantage and they had a 3-games-to-1 lead in the Series, putting them one win away from advancing to the World Series. The Giants had Barry Zito on the mound.

The 2002 Cy Young Award winner had been left off the Giants' 2010 postseason roster after struggling during his time in San Francisco. But Zito, in his 174th start in a Giants' uniform, stepped up his game when it mattered most. His 7.2 shutout innings ensured that the Giants lived to play another day, and sent the series back to San Francisco. His outing also inspired a Twitter trend before his start, calling on fans to #RallyZito.

GAME 6, OCT. 21
GIANTS 6, CARDINALS 1

THE REMATCH OF the Game 2 starters, Chris Carpenter against Ryan Vogelsong, went much the same way as the first Giants victory of the series. Carpenter was chased from the game after allowing five runs — three of which were unearned — in four innings and Vogelsong earned the win for his strong showing. The only difference was that in Game 6, Vogelsong pitched even better. He struck out a career-high nine batters in seven innings, surrendering just one run in the sixth on Allen Craig's two-out single that scored Carlos Beltran.

The Giants' bats came alive early in the friendly confines of AT&T Park. In the bottom of the first, a double by Pablo Sandoval and a groundout by Buster Posey plated Marco Scutaro, who had walked earlier in the inning. First baseman Brandon Belt kicked off the second with a triple, later scoring on a swinging bunt by Vogelsong that was misplayed by St. Louis shortstop Pete Kozma. A double by Scutaro and a single by Sandoval capped a four-run frame. The Giants tacked on one more run in the sixth before the bullpen closed out the 6-1 win, sending the series to a decisive Game 7.

	1	2	3	4	5	6	7	8	9	R	H	E
ST. LOUIS	0	0	0	0	0	1	0	0	0	1	5	1
SAN FRANCISCO	1	4	0	0	0	0	0	1	x	6	9	1

WP: Vogelsong LP: C. Carpenter

Vogelsong recorded his second win of the series in the high-pressure elimination Game 6 with seven brilliant innings.

"THE FANS HERE BRING IT ALL THE TIME. IT'S AMAZING. WHEN I WAS STANDING ON THE MOUND TONIGHT AND THEY WERE CHEERING 'VOGEY,' IT JUST MADE ME WANT TO GET THE JOB DONE FOR THEM, MADE ME WANT TO DIG DOWN A LITTLE BIT. THE THINGS THAT THEY ARE DOING FOR ME AS FAR AS THEIR CHEERS AND THE CHANTS ARE MAKING THIS SOMETHING THAT I'M NEVER, EVER GOING TO FORGET. AND I CAN'T THANK THEM ENOUGH FOR THAT."

Ryan Vogelsong

Belt's leadoff triple in the second inning jump-started a four-run frame that gave the Giants an untouchable lead.

GAME 7, OCT. 22
GIANTS 9, CARDINALS 0

IT WAS POURING rain by the time the Giants and their fans at AT&T Park celebrated the team's 22nd National League pennant. But no one on the field or in the stands seemed to care. The Giants' rousing 9-0 victory over the Cardinals — their record-tying sixth straight while facing elimination — capped a stunning rally to overcome a 3-games-to-1 series deficit. And for the fans, it was their first opportunity to celebrate their team clinching at home since the 2002 NLCS.

Right-handed ace Matt Cain rounded out the triumvirate of spotless performances from Giants pitchers, tossing 5.2 scoreless innings before leaving the game in the capable hands of San Francisco's bullpen. As for the offense, over the final three games of the NLCS, the Giants outscored the Cardinals, 20-1, and in Game 7, everyone got in on the action. All nine starting players — even Cain — contributed to the 14-hit affair, perhaps none more spectacularly than Hunter Pence, whose bases-loaded, broken-bat double incited a five-run third inning, and NLCS MVP Marco Scutaro, who produced his sixth multi-hit game of the series.

	1	2	3	4	5	6	7	8	9		R	H	E
----------------	---	---	---	---	---	---	---	---	---		---	---	---
ST. LOUIS	0	0	0	0	0	0	0	0	0		0	7	2
SAN FRANCISCO	1	1	5	0	0	0	1	1	x		9	14	0

WP: Cain LP: Lohse
HR: SF: Belt

Teammates rushed onto the field to celebrate with Sergio Romo and Buster Posey after the final out in the ninth sent San Francisco to the World Series.

Pence's unique approach to hitting got even quirkier in Game 7, with a double that hit his bat three separate times before finding a hole up the middle.

"THESE GUYS DESERVE ALL THE CREDIT. THEY WERE DE-TERMINED NOT TO GO HOME. THEY HAD THAT NEVER-SAY-DIE ATTITUDE. HUNTER PENCE DID A GREAT JOB OF KEEPING THEM PUMPED-UP. THEY WERE PLAYING FOR EACH OTHER. THEY WERE DETERMINED AND IT SHOWED. AND, OF COURSE, OUR FANS JUST DID NOT WANT TO GO HOME." Bruce Bochy

GAME 7, OCT. 22
GIANTS 9, CARDINALS 0

After a game in which he had two RBI, two runs scored and caught the final out, Scutaro celebrated his NLCS MVP win and his first trip to the World Series.

Romo (center) and his Giants teammates celebrated in the rain at AT&T Park after sealing their second World Series appearance in three years.

MOST VALUABLE ACQUISITION

MARCO SCUTARO TILTED his head back in the rain, literally soaking it all in. Moments later, the 36-year-old veteran of six teams caught the final out of the 9-0 Game 7 win. With that, the Giants were NL champions, headed to the World Series. It was a fitting end to a series that showcased the talents of players on both scrappy teams, but none more so than the MVP. Scutaro came to San Francisco from Colorado in late July and played the best baseball of his career, batting .362 in 61 games for his new team. But even that paled in comparison to his NLCS performance. After taking a hard slide from Matt Holliday in Game 2, Scutaro stepped up his production, ending the series with a .500 average and a postseason series record-tying 14 hits.

GAME 1, OCT. 24
GIANTS 8, TIGERS 3

GAME 1 TURNED out to be historic. But what it started out to be was a night when everything seemed to go the Giants' way.

Although the Tigers sent out ace Justin Verlander, who struck out four batters in an uncharacteristically short four-inning outing, San Francisco managed to jump out to an early 1-0 lead on a Pablo Sandoval homer in the bottom of the first. That was just the beginning of a night that saw the top four hitters in the Giants' line-up — Angel Pagan, Marco Scutaro, Sandoval and Buster Posey — go 10 for 16 and cross the plate for seven of the team's eight runs. Four of those came on Sandoval's record-tying three-longball performance in as many consecutive at-bats, making him just the fourth player ever to go deep three times in one Fall Classic game.

The Giants also scored by conjuring up their share of two-out magic throughout the affair, coming back to score seemingly every time they were on the verge of collapse. Pagan's two-out double off the third-base bag in the bottom of the third sparked a three-run rally that was capped by Sandoval's second homer; Kung Fu Panda's first blast also came with two down.

San Francisco's offense cleared the way for Barry Zito and a contingent of Giants relievers — including Tim Lincecum, who entered in the fifth and provided 2.1 innings of no-hit ball — to stymie the Tigers. Not all of the Detroit bats were silent, though, as the club got on the board in the sixth, and Jhonny Peralta tacked on a pair of runs with a two-run blast in the ninth.

But just as a light rain began to fall in AT&T Park — as it had two nights earlier when the Giants clinched their second National League pennant in three years — Jeremy Affeldt came in to close out the contest and give the Giants the first win of the 2012 Fall Classic.

	1	2	3	4	5	6	7	8	9	R	H	E
DETROIT	0	0	0	0	0	1	0	0	2	3	8	0
SAN FRANCISCO	1	0	3	1	1	0	2	0	x	8	11	0

WP: Zito **LP:** Verlander **HR:** DET: Peralta; SF: Sandoval 3

Sandoval joined Babe Ruth, Reggie Jackson and Albert Pujols as the only players ever to hit three home runs in a single World Series game.

In the third inning, Sandoval took Verlander deep for the second time. His two-run shot into the seats in left field gave the Giants a 4-0 lead.

GAME 1, OCT. 24
GIANTS 8, TIGERS 3

Zito (above, left) pitched brilliantly for his second start in a row, limiting Detroit to just one run in 5.2 innings; Verlander (above, right) struggled in his third career World Series start, as he lasted a season-low four innings and allowed five runs; Gregor Blanco (opposite, top) made a pair of diving catches in left field to help stifle the Tigers' offense; Austin Jackson doubled and came home on a Miguel Cabrera single for Detroit's first run of the game in the sixth.

"I BATTLED IN SEPTEMBER TO MAKE THE POSTSEASON ROSTER. THE LAST THING I WOULD HAVE EXPECTED AT THAT POINT WAS TO BE STARTING GAME 1." Barry Zito

PANDA-MONIUM

TWO YEARS AFTER the Giants opened what became their first victorious World Series in San Francisco, they were back. Same venue, same cast of characters, same goal. And, as it turns out, same outcome.

One thing that certainly wasn't the same, though, was Pablo Sandoval. The third baseman didn't play in Game 1 of the 2010 World Series, and in fact had just three plate appearances in that Fall Classic. But in Game 1 of this World Series, he turned in a three–home run outing that will go down in history.

"In 2010, I didn't get a chance to play too much," the Giants hero said. "I'm enjoying this World Series. I'm enjoying all of the moments. You never know when it's going to happen again."

Indeed, no one could have known when history was going to be made again, as only Babe Ruth, Reggie Jackson and Albert Pujols have hit as many longballs as Sandoval in a World Series game.

"After the third one I looked at him and said, 'Wow,'" said teammate Buster Posey. "And he was just smiling."

GAME 1, OCT. 24
GIANTS 8, TIGERS 3

Delmon Young watched Sandoval's second homer of the night fly over the left-field wall in the third inning.

Tigers players stood in front of their dugout holding placards as part of a Stand Up To Cancer tribute after the bottom of the fifth inning.

GAME 1, OCT. 24
GIANTS 8, TIGERS 3

"HITTING THREE HOME RUNS AT ANY POINT IN THE SEASON IS IMPRESSIVE, BUT ESPECIALLY TO DO IT ON THIS STAGE." Buster Posey on Pablo Sandoval

GAME 2, OCT. 25
GIANTS 2, TIGERS 0

A NIGHT AFTER playing power ball, the Giants won in an entirely different fashion in Game 2. In a contest that was wonderfully pitched by both teams and scoreless through six-and-a-half innings, executing the finer points of the game proved to be the difference. Giants starter Madison Bumgarner mostly cruised through seven frames, but Detroit did have its chances right from the beginning. After Prince Fielder was hit by a pitch, Delmon Young ripped a double into the left-field corner, and on the throw, Gregor Blanco overshot the cutoff man. But Marco Scutaro, trailing right behind, grabbed the ball and fired it to home to just barely nail Fielder. "That could be the turning point of the game right there," said Sergio Romo. "It could have been the first run." It was the first of many chances the Giants would have to show off their fundamentals — from great defensive plays to a bunt to a key stolen base.

Bumgarner and Tigers starter Doug Fister dueled from there until the bottom of the seventh. In that frame, a single, walk and bunt single by Blanco loaded the bases with no outs. Detroit Manager Jim Leyland opted to concede the run and play at double play depth, and he got what he wanted — a 6-4-3 twin killing — but the Giants grabbed a 1-0 lead. Three walks from two different Tigers relievers put San Francisco in business again in the ninth, and a Hunter Pence sac fly plated a run to increase the lead to 2-0.

Sergio Romo preserved the victory by throwing a perfect ninth inning that gave the Giants a 2-games-to-none Series edge. "The faith my teammates have in me is unreal," Romo said. "It's unwavering." Unwavering would also be a fair way to describe the near-perfect ball that his team had played from the end of the NLCS through the first two games of the World Series.

	1	2	3	4	5	6	7	8	9	R	H	E
DETROIT	0	0	0	0	0	0	0	0	0	0	2	0
SAN FRANCISCO	0	0	0	0	0	0	1	1	x	2	5	0

WP: Bumgarner LP: Fister SV: Romo

With the game locked in a scoreless tie, Blanco laid down a bunt single in the seventh to load the bases and set up a run-scoring double play.

In a pivotal moment, home plate umpire Dan Iassogna ruled Blanco's bunt fair, giving him an infield single.

"THAT BUNT SINGLE WAS EXCITING. I WAS JUMPING UP AND DOWN WHEN I GOT TO FIRST. IN THE WORLD SERIES, IN THAT SITUATION, IT WAS THE BEST BUNT EVER FOR ME."
Gregor Blanco

GAME 2, OCT. 25
GIANTS 2, TIGERS 0

Clockwise from above: Despite diving into first base, Scutaro was beaten by the throw; Brandon Crawford shut down the Tigers' attempt at a fourth-inning rally by tagging out Omar Infante on an attempted steal for the final out of the frame; Romo pitched a perfect ninth to earn his first World Series save.

"THE TIGERS ARE THE BEST IN THE WORLD AND THEY GOT HERE FOR A REASON, SO YOU'VE GOT TO TRY TO GET THEM ONE-TWO-THREE. THESE GUYS ARE UNREAL." Sergio Romo

GAME 2, OCT. 25
GIANTS 2, TIGERS 0

The Tigers' best chance to score came when Fielder, who had walked, tried to come home on Young's double. But the throw to the plate just barely beat him, and Buster Posey tagged him out to preserve the shutout.

BOUNCES

MAKE NO MISTAKE, the Tigers did not hit in the first two games of this Fall Classic, while the Giants not only pitched exceptionally well but also took advantage of seemingly every situation. It didn't hurt, though, that every bounce seemed to go their way, and three of those — all involving the third-base line — had a lot to do with the outcome of these games.

In Game 1, with the Giants clinging to just a 1-0 third-inning lead, Angel Pagan's roller down the line dinged off the third-base bag and trickled into left field for a leadoff double that set the stage for a three-run inning.

The following day, in the top of the second, as Delmon Young's double headed down the third-base line, the ball struck a part of the wall the jutted out into foul territory, which caused it to shoot back toward left fielder Gregor Blanco as Prince Fielder rounded third and headed for the plate. If the ball had hugged the line all the way to the corner, Fielder would have had more time to score and give the Tigers their first lead of the Series. But as it turned out, Blanco grabbed the ball and was able to start the relay that nailed Fielder at the plate by inches.

"We could have been on the other side of both of those plays, and we could be talking about two different games here," said Giants pitcher Ryan Vogelsong. "Sometimes the ball bounces your way."

Blanco would be involved in one more that's-the-way-the-ball-bounces moment in the seventh inning. With runners on first and second and no outs in a scoreless tie, Blanco laid down a one-strike bunt. Tigers catcher Gerald Laird and pitcher Drew Smyly let the ball roll until it came to a stop just inside the third-base line. That set up a based-loaded situation, allowing the Giants to take a 1-0 lead on a subsequent double play ball. The win gave them a two-game Series advantage.

GAME 3, OCT. 27
GIANTS 2, TIGERS 0

DOWN 2 GAMES to none heading into the third contest, the Tigers still had hope. The Series was heading to the friendly confines of Detroit's Comerica Park and the team was sure its bats would heat up.

But just as in the first two outings, the Tigers fell flat, stymied again by dominant Giants pitching. For the second game in a row, Detroit was unable to score, this time against 35-year-old Ryan Vogelsong, who two years before was released from a Minor League contract with the Los Angeles Angels while the Giants were competing against Texas for their 2010 championship. In 5.2 innings of work in Game 3, Vogelsong limited the lethal Tigers offense to just five hits, while Tim Lincecum and Sergio Romo came on to provide no-hit relief.

Meanwhile, the Giants got on the board early in the game, scoring two runs in the top of the second — and that would be all the offense they'd need. As was the case throughout the Series' early games, San Francisco capitalized on every opportunity — in this case, a walk to enthusiastic team leader Hunter Pence, a stolen base, a wild pitch and a Gregor Blanco triple — to give the pitching staff all the support it would need with a 2-0 lead that silenced the packed Comerica Park crowd.

Pence, the Giants right fielder and No. 5 hitter who went 2 for 3 in the game and scored a run, summed up his team's success. "Everyone seems to be in the right place," he said. "We have to continue to play like there's no tomorrow."

But there certainly was a tomorrow on the horizon — one that could seal the championship for the Giants and leave the Tigers empty-handed. That reality was not lost on many members of the Detroit club.

"The best approach is being able to get the mistakes — to take advantage of opportunities," conceded the Tigers' Alex Avila. "We're not doing that."

	1	2	3	4	5	6	7	8	9	R	H	E
SAN FRANCISCO	0	2	0	0	0	0	0	0	0	2	7	1
DETROIT	0	0	0	0	0	0	0	0	0	0	5	1

WP: Vogelsong LP: Sanchez
SV: Romo

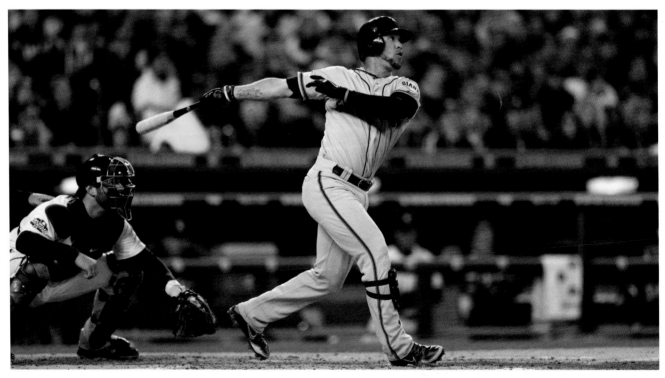

Blanco's RBI triple in the top of the second proved to be all the offense the Giants would need to secure a win and a 3-games-to-none Series lead.

Continuing to contribute out of the bullpen, Lincecum pitched 2.1 innings of no-hit ball in middle relief to preserve the Giants' lead.

"GOOD PITCHING WILL ALWAYS OUTWEIGH GOOD HITTING."
Brian Wilson

GAME 3, OCT. 27
GIANTS 2, TIGERS 0

Sandoval swung a hot bat throughout the Series, adding a double in the eighth inning of Game 3.

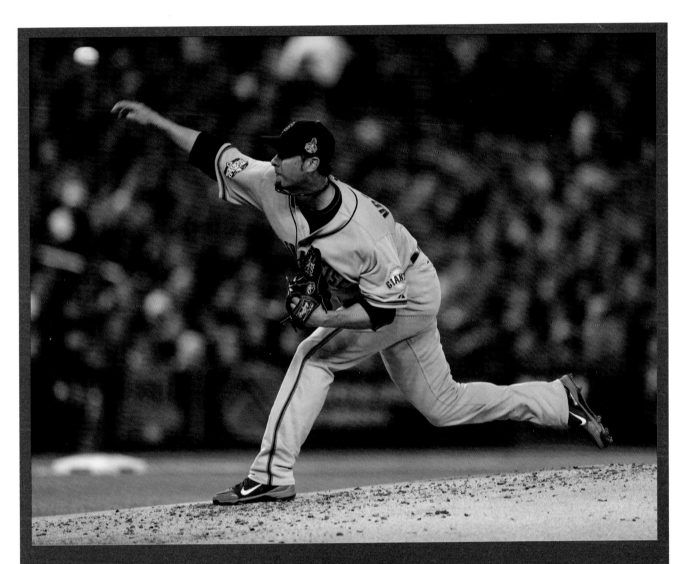

WORTH THE WAIT

THE FIRST THREE games of the 2012 World Series saw the Giants outscore the Tigers 12-3. And in a Series that was reminiscent of the 2010 Fall Classic for the Giants' dominance on the hill, much of that success resulted from razor-sharp pitching.

Starter Ryan Vogelsong was the force behind San Francisco's Game 3 win. After leaving the contest with two outs in the fifth, Vogelsong boasted a 2012 postseason ERA that stood at 1.13 — the lowest over at least 24 playoff innings since Curt Schilling posted a 1.12 mark during Arizona's 2001 title run.

"It's my first World Series," said Vogelsong, who was stuck in the Minors as recently as last April. "I've been waiting for this since I was 5 years old, and I wasn't going to go down without a fight, that's for sure."

And when he did leave the game, relievers Tim Lincecum and Sergio Romo stepped in to keep the Tigers at bay. "They've been very competitive games," said San Francisco reliever Jeremy Affeldt. "You're seeing what good pitching does. But you're also seeing the importance of bullpens. When Timmy comes in, it doesn't get any easier."

GAME 3, OCT. 27
GIANTS 2, TIGERS 0

Sandoval, the eventual MVP of the Series, readied for one of his nine at-bats at Comerica Park.

GAME 4, OCT. 28
GIANTS 4, TIGERS 3

	1	2	3	4	5	6	7	8	9	10	R	H	E
SAN FRANCISCO	0	1	0	0	0	2	0	0	0	1	4	9	0
DETROIT	0	0	2	0	0	1	0	0	0	0	3	5	1

WP: Casilla LP: Coke SV: Romo
HR: SF: Posey; DET: Cabrera, Young

Belt put the Giants on the board early in their clinching game with an RBI triple in the top of the second that knocked in Pence.

THE GIANTS DROPPED the first two games of the Division Series against the Reds. Then they fell behind 3-games-to-1 against the Cardinals in the NLCS. So it was fair for their fans to wonder how safe they should feel when the team jumped out ahead of the Tigers in the World Series, eventually going into Game 4 with a commanding lead. But the fearless team had ace Matt Cain on the hill, and San Francisco jumped on the scoreboard in the second inning — a

great sign since the club had gone 9-1 when scoring first in the postseason. This time, a Hunter Pence ground-rule double followed by a triple from rookie Brandon Belt — his first hit of the Fall Classic — gave San Francisco a 1-0 lead before fans at Comerica Park even had the chance to feel the chill of the rainy, 45-degree weather.

The Tigers roared back, however, when Miguel Cabrera launched a two-run homer in the bottom of the third to give them their first lead of the entire Series. The blast also meant that Cabrera had reached base in all 24 of the postseason games he has played as a member of the Tigers; he has reached safely in 37 of 41 career postseason contests overall.

But the Giants, too, had an MVP candidate in the lineup, and that man, catcher Buster Posey, belted a two-run homer of his own in the top of the sixth to regain the lead for the Giants, 3-2. This World Series marked the fourth time that each league's batting champ have met in the Fall Classic, and Cabrera and Posey hoped that they'd become the first pair of World Series foes since 1988 to capture league MVP honors.

"We went through a lot of ups and downs — a lot of bumps in the road — but we never gave up," said outfielder Angel Pagan. "We wanted to get it done."

Unfortunately for the Tigers, the Giants would meet their goal in a rush. A Delmon Young longball in the bottom of the sixth tied the score again, but when the contest entered extra innings, the outcome was never in doubt in the San Francisco dugout. Ryan Theriot led off the 10th with a single, then Brandon Crawford bunted him over before Tigers reliever Phil Coke struck out Pagan to bring up NLCS hero Marco Scutaro.

"It was a moment that you really couldn't have written out much better," Pence said. "When Theriot was on second, we were yelling in the dugout that he had scored the game-winning run in the College World Series. And Scutaro was up. We just had a good feeling about the moment."

Scutaro laced a two-out RBI single that proved to be the game winner after Sergio Romo struck out the side in the bottom of the 10th. It marked his third save of the World Series and gave the Giants their seventh title. Of 24 teams that have taken a 3-0 Fall Classic lead, 21 of them have now closed it out in Game 4. The Giants have lost just one game in their last two World Series appearances, and they ended the 2012 postseason with seven straight wins.

Cain started all three clinching games in the Giants' 2012 postseason, pitching seven innings of three-run ball in the final World Series game.

GAME 4, OCT. 28
GIANTS 4, TIGERS 3

"I CAN'T BELIEVE IT. I'M EXCITED RIGHT NOW. THANK YOU TO MY TEAM, THANK YOU TO GIANTS FANS — THANK YOU FOR EVERYTHING." Jose Mijares

"I've never really been a part of any other group that bought in as much as we did," said Pence. "It didn't matter if you had differences anywhere else in the clubhouse, we loved every moment of it. It just speaks to the character of the people that put us together, and their intelligence. A tremendous amount of credit goes to [Manager Bruce] Bochy because he's the orchestrator. He pushes you, he gives you every opportunity to get the best out of you, he encourages you — he knows how to push the right buttons."

Added Pagan, "It's a special feeling to be out there. It's a long year. You get ready for the season knowing that you have a good chance to be in the postseason, you get to the postseason, and we were against the wall twice, and now we win the World Series — it's crazy."

Triple Crown winner Cabrera briefly gave Tigers fans hope with a two-run blast in the bottom of the third that gave Detroit its first lead of the Series.

Posey (above) reclaimed the lead for the Giants with a two-run shot in the sixth; Young tied the game with his own homer in the bottom of the frame.

BIGGEST GIANT OF THEM ALL

WHEN ALL WAS said and done and the Giants hoisted the gold flag-lined trophy, Pablo Sandoval cradled one of his own.

Walking around in the aftermath of his team's second World Series victory in three years — the first of which he barely took part in — Sandoval had the look of a man who was in awe of it all.

The Panda made his case for Series MVP beginning with his first Fall Classic at-bat — a line-drive homer off Tigers ace Justin Verlander. He added two more long-balls that day, going 4 for 4 with four RBI and three runs scored.

"I still can't believe that game," the third baseman said. "It's the game of your dreams. You don't want to wake up."

Over the next three contests, Sandoval's bat never cooled off. By the time the sweep was complete, he had tallied eight hits in 16 at-bats, posting a monstrous 1.654 OPS in the World Series.

"He got hot at the right time for us," said Giants Manager Bruce Bochy. "I couldn't be happier, prouder for him. I know it was a tough time in 2010 when he got relegated to the bench. He really wanted to shine on this stage."

GAME 4, OCT. 28
GIANTS 4, TIGERS 3

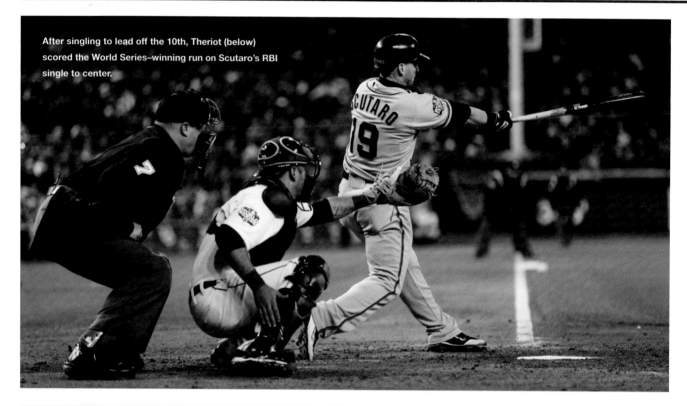

After singling to lead off the 10th, Theriot (below) scored the World Series–winning run on Scutaro's RBI single to center.

"THE PEOPLE THAT ARE HERE WITH ME, MINUS A COUPLE THAT COULDN'T MAKE THE TRIP, ARE EXACTLY THE ONES THAT I WANT. IT MAKES IT THAT MUCH MORE SPECIAL TO BE ABLE TO SHARE IT WITH MY FRIENDS AND FAMILY BECAUSE THEY LIVE AND DIE WITH EVERY GAME JUST LIKE I DO." Ryan Vogelsong

"I'M VERY GRATEFUL TO BE A PART OF THIS CLUB AND VERY HUMBLE TO BE A PART OF THIS MOMENT. WE BOUGHT INTO SOMETHING YOU DON'T SEE HAPPEN VERY OFTEN. WE BOUGHT INTO PLAYING FOR EACH OTHER, LOVING PLAYING FOR EACH OTHER, AND IT'S VERY UNIQUE." Hunter Pence

GAME 4, OCT. 28
GIANTS 4, TIGERS 3

On the field and in the clubhouse, Giants players celebrated their World Series sweep, which capped an incredible postseason run and brought a second championship in three years to San Francisco.

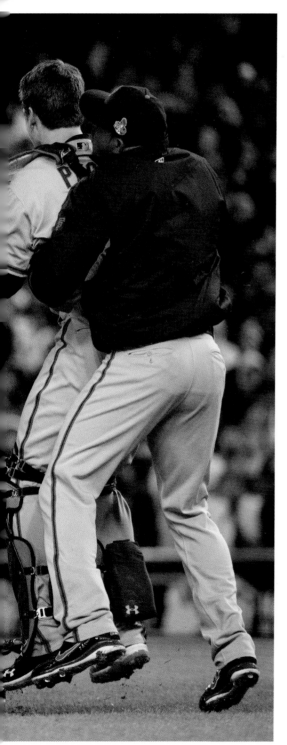

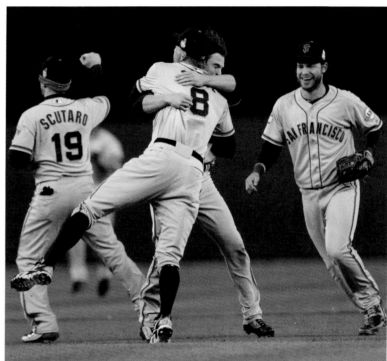

GAME 4, OCT. 28
GIANTS 4, TIGERS 3

In the bottom of the 10th, Romo froze Cabrera on a fastball that gave the closer the save and the Giants a World Series championship.

POSTSEASON STATS

NO.	PLAYER	W	L	ERA	SO	BB	SV
PITCHERS							
41	Jeremy Affeldt	0	0	0.00	10	3	0
40	Madison Bumgarner	1	2	6.00	14	4	0
18	Matt Cain	2	2	3.60	20	7	0
46	Santiago Casilla	1	0	1.29	8	1	0
70	George Kontos	0	0	6.75	2	1	0
55	Tim Lincecum	1	1	2.55	20	5	0
49	Javier Lopez	0	0	0.00	4	2	0
50	Jose Mijares	0	0	10.12	4	2	0
59	Guillermo Mota	0	0	21.60	3	0	0
54	Sergio Romo	1	0	0.84	9	1	4
32	Ryan Vogelsong	3	0	1.09	21	10	0
75	Barry Zito	2	0	1.69	13	6	0

NO.	PLAYER	AB	H	AVG	HR	RBI	OBP
CATCHERS							
28	Buster Posey	60	12	.200	3	9	.294
29	Hector Sanchez	11	1	.091	0	0	.231
INFIELDERS							
13	Joaquin Arias	8	3	.375	0	0	.375
9	Brandon Belt	49	9	.184	1	3	.286
35	Brandon Crawford	46	10	.217	0	7	.321
17	Aubrey Huff	9	1	.111	0	0	.200
48	Pablo Sandoval	66	24	.364	6	13	.386
19	Marco Scutaro	64	21	.328	0	8	.377
5	Ryan Theriot	10	3	.300	0	3	.364
OUTFIELDERS							
7	Gregor Blanco	51	12	.235	1	5	.339
12	Xavier Nady	5	0	.000	0	0	.167
16	Angel Pagan	69	13	.188	2	6	.230
8	Hunter Pence	62	13	.210	1	4	.231

POSTSEASON HISTORY

After winning 105 regular-season games, the Giants captured their first championship with a 4-games-to-1 World Series victory in 1905.

1905*
WORLD SERIES

FOLLOWING A 1904 Giants team that won 106 games in a year the World Series was not played, the 1905 Giants went 105-48 during the regular season behind a dominant pitching staff led by 25-year-old Christy Mathewson. They faced off against the 92-win Athletics in the World Series, where the Hall-of-Fame pitcher hurled three Fall Classic gems that collectively rank as the greatest pitching performance in Series history. The right-hander began the Series against the Athletics with a four-hit shutout in Game 1, a performance he replicated in Game 3. Pitching on one day's rest in Game 5, Mathewson hurled his third complete-game shutout of the Series, which still stands as a Fall Classic record, to give the Giants their first title.

GIANTS 4, PHILADELPHIA ATHLETICS 1
Oct. 9 Giants 3 at Athletics 0
Oct. 10 Athletics 3 at Giants 0
Oct. 12 Giants 9 at Athletics 0
Oct. 13 Athletics 0 at Giants 1
Oct. 14 Athletics 0 at Giants 2

*Denotes Championship Season

1911
WORLD SERIES
PHILADELPHIA ATHLETICS 4, GIANTS 2

Oct. 14 Athletics 1 at Giants 2
Oct. 16 Giants 1 at Athletics 3
Oct. 17 Athletics 3 at Giants 2
Oct. 24 Giants 2 at Athletics 4
Oct. 25 Athletics 3 at Giants 4
Oct. 26 Giants 2 at Athletics 13

1912
WORLD SERIES
BOSTON RED SOX 4, GIANTS 3

Oct. 8 Red Sox 4 at Giants 3
Oct. 9 Giants 6 at Red Sox 6
Oct. 10 Giants 2 at Red Sox 1
Oct. 11 Red Sox 3 at Giants 1
Oct. 12 Giants 1 at Red Sox 2
Oct. 14 Red Sox 2 at Giants 5
Oct. 15 Giants 11 at Red Sox 4
Oct. 16 Giants 2 at Red Sox 3

1913
WORLD SERIES
PHILADELPHIA ATHLETICS 4, GIANTS 1

Oct. 7 Athletics 6 at Giants 4
Oct. 8 Giants 3 at Athletics 0
Oct. 9 Athletics 8 at Giants 2
Oct. 10 Giants 5 at Athletics 6
Oct. 11 Athletics 3 at Giants 1

1917
WORLD SERIES
CHICAGO WHITE SOX 4, GIANTS 2

Oct. 6 Giants 1 at White Sox 2
Oct. 7 Giants 2 at White Sox 7
Oct. 10 White Sox 0 at Giants 2
Oct. 11 White Sox 0 at Giants 5
Oct. 13 Giants 5 at White Sox 8
Oct. 15 White Sox 4 at Giants 2

The Giants topped their crosstown rival Yankees in the 1921 World Series.

1921*
WORLD SERIES

THE GIANTS OF the 1910s failed to translate their regular-season success into a championship, with four teams losing the World Series after posting 98-plus-win seasons. In 1921, the franchise finally broke through, topping the Babe Ruth–led Yankees in the first Subway Series and last best-of-nine Series in Fall Classic history. With an offense paced by first baseman George "High Pockets" Kelly, the Giants finished first in the league in runs, but relied on strong pitching to close out their crosstown rivals in eight games. Twenty-game winner Art Nehf capped the victory by throwing a complete-game shutout in the clincher. All eight games were played at the Polo Grounds — the first time in history that each World Series game was played at the same site.

GIANTS 5, NEW YORK YANKEES 3
Oct. 5 Yankees 3 at Giants 0

Giants catcher Heinie Groh tagged out Ruth during the 1922 Series.

A trio of hurlers, led by Hubbell (center), pitched the Giants to a 1933 title.

Oct. 6 Giants 0 at Yankees 3
Oct. 7 Yankees 5 at Giants 13
Oct. 9 Giants 4 at Yankees 2
Oct. 10 Yankees 3 at Giants 1
Oct. 11 Giants 8 at Yankees 5
Oct. 12 Yankees 1 at Giants 2
Oct. 13 Giants 1 at Yankees 0

1922*
WORLD SERIES

THE REMATCH OF the previous World Series resulted in a clean sweep, but not without controversy. The thrilling Game 2 ended in a tie after 10 innings — the third and final tied game in Fall Classic history — when the umpires inexplicably called it, citing darkness although it was only 4:45 p.m. A near riot ensued among the 37,020 fans at the Polo Grounds, with customers demanding their money back. When play resumed the next day, the Giants took command. That year's offensive star, outfielder Irish Meusel, drove in seven runs in the Series after knocking in 132 during the regular season. The Giants scored three in the bottom of the eighth inning of Game 5, as Art Nehf once again sealed the title with a complete-game win.

GIANTS 4, NEW YORK YANKEES 0
Oct. 4 Yankees 2 at Giants 3
Oct. 5 Giants 3 at Yankees 3
Oct. 6 Yankees 0 at Giants 3
Oct. 7 Giants 4 at Yankees 3
Oct. 8 Yankees 3 at Giants 5

1923
WORLD SERIES
NEW YORK YANKEES 4, GIANTS 2
Oct. 10 Giants 5 at Yankees 4
Oct. 11 Yankees 4 at Giants 2
Oct. 12 Giants 1 at Yankees 0
Oct. 13 Yankees 8 at Giants 4
Oct. 14 Giants 1 at Yankees 8
Oct. 15 Yankees 6 at Giants 4

1924
WORLD SERIES
WASHINGTON SENATORS 4, GIANTS 3
Oct. 4 Giants 4 at Senators 3
Oct. 5 Giants 3 at Senators 4
Oct. 6 Senators 4 at Giants 6
Oct. 7 Senators 7 at Giants 4
Oct. 8 Senators 2 at Giants 6
Oct. 9 Giants 1 at Senators 2
Oct. 10 Giants 3 at Senators 4

1933*
WORLD SERIES

THE 1933 SEASON marked the first one since 1901 played without Manager John McGraw, who retired with 2,763 career wins — a record total that would eventually be surpassed by Connie Mack — and 10 pennants. First baseman Bill Terry stepped in as a player-manager, while Hall of Famer Mel Ott carried the offensive load and left-hander Carl Hubbell dominated on the mound

*Denotes Championship Season

during both the regular season and the World Series. Ott knocked seven hits, including two homers, in 18 Fall Classic at-bats, while Hubbell won Games 1 and 4, allowing just 13 hits and no earned runs over 20 innings. An extra-inning victory at Griffith Stadium in Game 5 ended the 99-win Senators' surprising season.

GIANTS 4, WASHINGTON SENATORS 1
Oct. 3 Senators 2 at Giants 4
Oct. 4 Senators 1 at Giants 6
Oct. 5 Giants 0 at Senators 4
Oct. 6 Giants 2 at Senators 1
Oct. 7 Giants 4 at Senators 3

1936
WORLD SERIES
NEW YORK YANKEES 4, GIANTS 2
Sept. 30 Yankees 1 at Giants 6
Oct. 2 Yankees 18 at Giants 4
Oct. 3 Giants 1 at Yankees 2
Oct. 4 Giants 2 at Yankees 5
Oct. 5 Giants 5 at Yankees 4
Oct. 6 Yankees 13 at Giants 5

1937
WORLD SERIES
NEW YORK YANKEES 4, GIANTS 1
Oct. 6 Giants 1 at Yankees 8
Oct. 7 Giants 1 at Yankees 8
Oct. 8 Yankees 5 at Giants 1
Oct. 9 Yankees 3 at Giants 7
Oct. 10 Yankees 4 at Giants 2

1951
WORLD SERIES
NEW YORK YANKEES 4, GIANTS 2
Oct. 4 Giants 5 at Yankees 1
Oct. 5 Giants 1 at Yankees 3
Oct. 6 Yankees 2 at Giants 6
Oct. 8 Yankees 6 at Giants 2
Oct. 9 Yankees 13 at Giants 1
Oct. 10 Giants 3 at Yankees 4

1954*
WORLD SERIES
EVEN THOSE WHO weren't there on Sept. 29, 1954 are familiar with the images of Willie Mays racing to deep center field at the Polo Grounds and corralling the ball over his left shoulder to rob Cleveland's Vic Wertz of an extra-base hit. "The Catch" preserved a tie in the eighth inning of Game 1 and set the tone of the World Series. New York never looked back after that game, finishing off the favored Indians, who were coming off a 111-win regular season, in four games. Little-known outfielder Dusty Rhodes came up with several clutch pinch-hits to boost the Giants.

GIANTS 4, CLEVELAND INDIANS 0
Sept. 29 Indians 2 at Giants 5
Sept. 30 Indians 1 at Giants 3
Oct. 1 Giants 6 at Indians 2
Oct. 2 Giants 7 at Indians 4

Teammates greeted Rhodes in the dugout during the '54 Series sweep.

1962
WORLD SERIES
NEW YORK YANKEES 4, GIANTS 3
Oct. 4 Yankees 6 at Giants 2
Oct. 5 Yankees 0 at Giants 2
Oct. 7 Giants 2 at Yankees 3
Oct. 8 Giants 7 at Yankees 3
Oct. 10 Giants 3 at Yankees 5
Oct. 15 Yankees 2 at Giants 5
Oct. 16 Yankees 1 at Giants 0

1971

NLCS

PITTSBURGH PIRATES 3, GIANTS 1

Oct. 2 Pirates 4 at Giants 5
Oct. 3 Pirates 9 at Giants 4
Oct. 5 Giants 1 at Pirates 2
Oct. 6 Giants 5 at Pirates 9

1987

NLCS

ST. LOUIS CARDINALS 4, GIANTS 3

Oct. 6 Giants 3 at Cardinals 5
Oct. 7 Giants 5 at Cardinals 0
Oct. 9 Cardinals 6 at Giants 5
Oct. 10 Cardinals 2 at Giants 4
Oct. 11 Cardinals 3 at Giants 6
Oct. 13 Giants 0 at Cardinals 1
Oct. 14 Giants 0 at Cardinals 6

1989

NLCS

GIANTS 4, CHICAGO CUBS 1

Oct. 4 Giants 11 at Cubs 3
Oct. 5 Giants 5 at Cubs 9
Oct. 7 Cubs 4 at Giants 5
Oct. 8 Cubs 4 at Giants 6
Oct. 9 Cubs 2 at Giants 3

WORLD SERIES

OAKLAND ATHLETICS 4, GIANTS 0

Oct. 14 Giants 0 at Athletics 5
Oct. 15 Giants 1 at Athletics 5
Oct. 27 Athletics 13 at Giants 7
Oct. 28 Athletics 9 at Giants 6

1997

NLDS

FLORIDA MARLINS 3, GIANTS 0

Sept. 30 Giants 1 at Marlins 2
Oct. 1 Giants 6 at Marlins 7
Oct. 3 Marlins 6 at Giants 2

2000

NLDS

NEW YORK METS 3, GIANTS 1

Oct. 4 Mets 1 at Giants 5
Oct. 5 Mets 5 at Giants 4
Oct. 7 Giants 2 at Mets 3
Oct. 8 Giants 0 at Mets 4

2002

NLDS

GIANTS 3, ATLANTA BRAVES 2

Oct. 2 Giants 8 at Braves 5
Oct. 3 Giants 3 at Braves 7
Oct. 5 Braves 10 at Giants 2
Oct. 6 Braves 3 at Giants 8
Oct. 7 Giants 3 at Braves 1

NLCS

GIANTS 4, ST. LOUIS CARDINALS 1

OCT. 9 Giants 9 at Cardinals 6
Oct. 10 Giants 4 at Cardinals 1
Oct. 12 Cardinals 5 at Giants 4
Oct. 13 Cardinals 3 at Giants 4
Oct. 14 Cardinals 1 at Giants 2

WORLD SERIES

ANAHEIM ANGELS 4, GIANTS 3

Oct. 19 Giants 4 at Angels 3
Oct. 20 Giants 10 at Angels 11
Oct. 22 Angels 10 at Giants 4
Oct. 23 Angels 3 at Giants 4
Oct. 24 Angels 4 at Giants 16
Oct. 26 Giants 5 at Angels 6
Oct. 27 Giants 1 at Angels 4

2003

NLDS

FLORIDA MARLINS 3, GIANTS 1

Sept. 30 Marlins 0 at Giants 2
Oct. 1 Marlins 9 at Giants 5
Oct. 3 Giants 3 at Marlins 4
Oct. 4 Giants 6 at Marlins 7

Denotes Championship Season

Members of the 2010 Giants ran out to the mound to celebrate their title with then-rookie catcher Buster Posey and Wilson after the Series' final out.

2010*

NLDS
GIANTS 3, ATLANTA BRAVES 1
Oct. 7 Braves 0 at Giants 1
Oct. 8 Braves 5 at Giants 4
Oct. 10 Giants 3 at Braves 2
Oct. 11 Giants 3 at Braves 2

NLCS
GIANTS 4, PHILADELPHIA PHILLIES 2
Oct. 16 Giants 4 at Phillies 3
Oct. 17 Giants 1 at Phillies 6
Oct. 19 Phillies 0 at Giants 3
Oct. 20 Phillies 5 at Giants 6
Oct 21 Phillies 4 at Giants 2
Oct. 23 Giants 3 at Phillies 2

WORLD SERIES
OF ALL THE memories the Giants had given Bay Area faithful in their 50-plus years since moving to the West Coast, a World Series title was not one of them. In 2010, the ragtag Giants made history, becoming San Francisco's first champions of the baseball world.

Manager Bruce Bochy affectionately referred to his team as a bunch of "castoffs and misfits", but it was those castoffs and misfits who steamrolled through the playoffs, eventually beating the offensive goliath Texas Rangers in only five games to win the World Series.

A powerful rotation led by Tim Lincecum, a strong bullpen anchored by bearded closer Brian Wilson and a scrappy lineup that could hit in the clutch fired on all cylinders at exactly the right time, conjuring up Bay Area baseball magic.

GIANTS 4, TEXAS RANGERS 1
Oct. 27 Rangers 7 at Giants 11
Oct. 28 Rangers 0 at Giants 9
Oct. 30 Giants 2 at Rangers 4
Oct. 31 Giants 4 at Rangers 0
Nov. 1 Giants 3 at Rangers 1

Denotes Championship Season

Legendary musician Ray Charles sang
"America the Beautiful" before Game 2
of the 2001 World Series in Arizona. The
process of selecting performers begins
more than a month in advance.

ANTHEMS

THE WORLD SERIES is more than just a grand stage for Major League Baseball's two best teams. For top musical talent, it's a chance to perform the national anthem in front of a huge audience. Not surprisingly, the Fall Classic brings out some of the biggest names in music. The goal, according to MLB's Marla Miller, senior vice president for special events, is to award the assignment to a performer with national appeal and, ideally, a connection to the city that is hosting that particular game.

Performers tapped for the prestigious honor have ranged from former American Idol contestants Carrie Underwood and Philip Phillips to stars who appeal to an even younger generation, like Taylor Swift. Classic artists have certainly belted out The Star-Spangled Banner on the World Series stage, as well. The late Ray Charles, Patti LaBelle, James Taylor, Gloria Estefan, Melissa Etheridge, Billy Joel and Paul Simon are just a few of the names that have performed prior to the first pitch of the ballgame. Artists come from many genres of music, too, with country artists, rockers and, yes, even boy bands getting the chance to take center stage.

The selection of national anthem singers begins well in advance of the World Series. In mid-September, contending teams submit to MLB a list of performers who have an affinity for the team or a connection to the community. Some musical acts can perform only in certain cities on specific dates because of scheduling conflicts, but performers are usually honored to sing the anthem. For Games 5 through 7, MLB does not release the names of anthem singers until it's determined that each game will be necessary.

There's always the possibility of a last-minute change due to unforeseen circumstances. Before Game 5 of the 2008 World Series in Philadelphia, Daryl Hall of the band Hall & Oates came down with the flu. Hall, a Pennsylvania native and graduate of Temple University, turned to his longtime singing partner John Oates to pinch-hit. Oates, who didn't get the call at his home in Colorado until 8 a.m. the morning of Game 5, scrambled to make it to Philadelphia, just 25 miles from where he grew up in North Wales, Pa.

Except in those rare, last-minute situations, performers complete a rehearsal, generally around 1 p.m., to gauge their comfort level in the stadium, and also to give MLB officials an idea of how long the rendition of the anthem will last. This enables the TV network to plan the length of its pregame commercial break, hopefully down to the second. The rehearsals also help set the timing for things like flyovers and fireworks.

Performers typically arrive at the ballpark with managers, agents or other handlers. Major League Baseball also provides staffers and resident security agents to help the singers travel around the park smoothly. Anthem acts receive World Series–themed clothing and other souvenirs, and many stay for the game.

"You'll find that top-tier musical talent is always interested because of the promotional value and exposure," Miller said. "No matter how successful they are, it's not every day that you get a chance to perform at the World Series."

UNIFORMS

TEAMS ISSUE NEW uniforms for the World Series so that players aren't wearing beat-up clothing for baseball's showcase event. Official World Series patches are sewn onto two sets each of both home and away jerseys. Players, managers and coaches usually get to keep one set of each.

Officials from the New Era Cap Co., the official headwear provider of MLB since 1993, affix the World Series emblem to two hats for each player, manager and coach with a heavy-duty steam press machine at the site of the World Series.

Before Major League Baseball applied an authentication system, placing holograms on World Series jerseys and logging each item into a database, the presence of these patches helped authenticate jerseys when they reached the collectibles market.

Throughout the regular season, teams usually enlist the help of a seamstress, who will visit the clubhouses on an almost-daily basis to repair uniforms and create jerseys for newly acquired players. This involves sewing on numbers and nameplates. Once a team reaches the World Series, there's suddenly a huge sewing workload to personalize all the new jerseys. Often, teams employ not just their regular seamstress, but might also bring on additional assistance.

Given the late October schedule of the World Series, additional cold-weather clothing is often needed. Cold-weather caps, which featured built-in earflaps that folded down, much like the hunting headwear worn by cartoon character Elmer Fudd, debuted — and were greatly appreciated — during the 2008 Fall Classic. New Era first issued them during Spring Training before the 2008 season, but they were not worn on the field until Game 5 of the World Series in Philadelphia, when rain and cold forced the game to be suspended in the sixth inning for nearly 48 hours. By the time the game was stopped, nearly everyone in uniform had opted for the Elmer Fudd look.

In the Midwest, this style is known as a "Stormy Kromer," named for a former semi-pro baseball player named George "Stormy" Kromer, who worked as a locomotive engineer. In 1903, Kromer asked his wife, Ida, to modify one of his baseball hats for protection against the brutal wintertime winds. Railroad workers and police officers have worn the all-wool creation for years.

OFFICIAL WORLD SERIES PATCHES ARE SEWN ONTO TWO SETS OF BOTH HOME AND AWAY JERSEYS. PLAYERS, MANAGERS AND COACHES USUALLY GET TO KEEP ONE SET OF EACH.

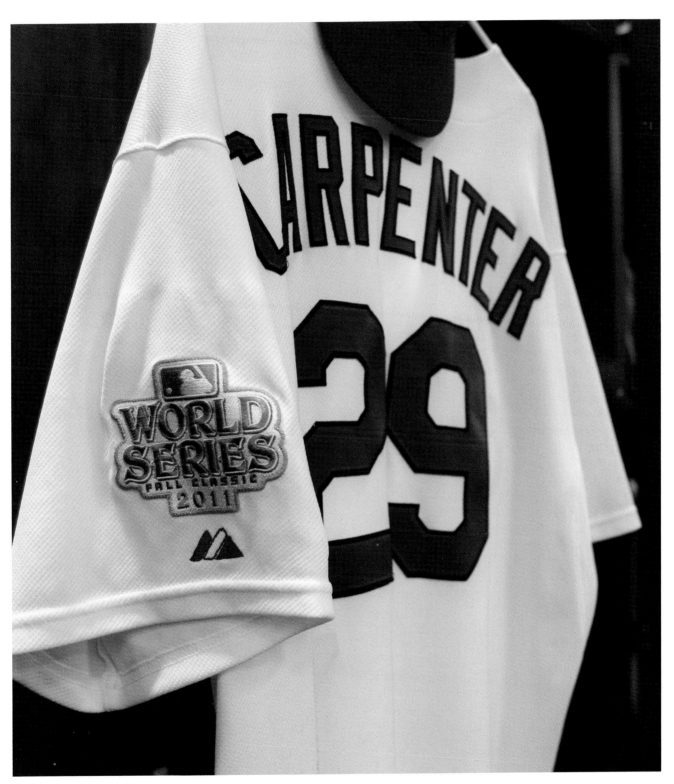

ROBERTO CLEMENTE AWARD

ONE OF BASEBALL'S most prestigious awards isn't just a recognition of on-field performance, statistics or win-loss records. The Roberto Clemente Award, presented by Chevrolet, is awarded prior to Game 3 of each World Series. It is given to the player who demonstrates the values that Clemente displayed in his commitment to helping others, in addition to his greatness on the field.

When the award was first bestowed by MLB in 1971, it was called the Commissioner's Award, but it was renamed in Clemente's honor in 1973 after the Pittsburgh Pirates outfielder died tragically in a plane crash while traveling to provide relief to earthquake victims in Nicaragua.

"As a national pastime and as a social institution, we in baseball have important social responsibilities that we gladly welcome," Commissioner Bud Selig said in 2008, while presenting the award to St. Louis' Albert Pujols. "Roberto Clemente is the symbol of our social awareness and our effort to give back to all the communities in which we play the game."

Each club nominates one of its own players for the award in September, and the winner is then selected from those 30 nominees. The past winners of the award represent some of baseball's most prominent names from the last four decades. The list is made up of several Hall of Famers and other well-respected contributors, including Dale Murphy, Brooks Robinson, Lou Brock, Rod Carew, Gary Carter, John Smoltz, Al Kaline, Willie Mays, Phil Niekro, Kirby Puckett, Cal Ripken Jr., Don Baylor, Ozzie Smith, Willie Stargell and Derek Jeter.

In 2001, Curt Schilling was helping the Arizona Diamondbacks to a World Series championship when he received the award. It was especially meaningful since he grew up a Pirates fan and the first game he attended in person was Clemente's last.

Several years before receiving the honor, Schilling vowed to use his platform as a Big Leaguer for something that would warrant consideration for the award. He eventually launched a foundation dedicated to curing ALS (Lou Gehrig's Disease).

"I looked at my wife when they were handing out the Clemente Award at the World Series in 1993, and I said to her, 'If I play long enough and I stay healthy enough, that's the one award I want to win before I'm done playing,'" Schilling said. "Because to win that award, it will not matter how many wins or strikeouts I have; I will have made a difference in peoples' lives."

Every year, Chevrolet donates to the winner's charity as well as to the Roberto Clemente Sports City in Puerto Rico — an organization that gives kids access to recreational sports facilities.

In 2006, Carlos Delgado received the Clemente Award for work with his foundation, Extra Bases, which assists underprivileged kids. Among other initiatives, the foundation puts together an annual pre-Thanksgiving feast for hundreds of homeless, underprivileged and handicapped children in Delgado's hometown of Aguadilla, Puerto Rico, where Delgado helps prepare and hand out the food. Like previous recipients of the award, Delgado was emotional upon receiving the honor from Commissioner Selig and Vera Clemente, Roberto's widow. The award carried special meaning for Delgado, who chose to wear No. 21 with the New York Mets in honor of Clemente.

"It is an extreme honor for me to be selected for an award that bears the name of Roberto Clemente. He was a Hall-of-Fame player and a Hall-of-Fame person," Delgado said. "Roberto's legacy to me is that it's an athlete's obligation to give back. That's what I have tried to do throughout my career."

Los Angeles Dodgers hurler Clayton Kershaw was awarded the 2012 Roberto Clemente Award.

PROGRAMS

THE OFFICIAL WORLD Series Program isn't just a guide to the Fall Classic and the teams competing for the championship. It's a 200-plus-page keepsake with two dozen feature-length stories and 75,000 words that chronicle World Series and baseball history, as well as current Big League trends. The content is written by some of baseball's best writers, including Tim Kurkjian, Jeff Passan and Peter Gammons.

"It's critical that the World Series Program is as up-to-date as possible," said Don Hintze, MLB's vice president of publishing and photos, whose department is in charge of producing all of MLB's special-event programs. "By waiting until the World Series matchup is determined, we're able to feature players from each participating team on the cover, as well as a postseason recap, which highlights how each team advanced to the Fall Classic. That helps make the programs more valuable to fans."

The World Series Program debuted along with the Fall Classic in 1903. Then, each team produced a volume for its home games that contained rosters and local advertisements. Entrepreneur and Polo Grounds concessionaire Harry M. Stevens is credited with publishing more than one-third of all World Series Programs before MLB took over the responsibility in 1974.

Features of the modern book include a scorecard as well as two sections of either eight, 16 or 32 pages produced by the participating clubs. These local sections include rosters, short player profiles, season recaps, brief features and accounts of any previous Fall Classic appearances. Mike McCormick, the editorial director for MLB, looks at the contending teams when assigning stories in August. In 2008, a story on first-time pennant contenders focusing on the Rays proved prescient when they advanced to the World Series. There are times, however, when a team like the 2007 Rockies comes out of nowhere late in the season, causing a last-minute scramble for content.

"The main goal is for this program to have a local feel when possible and an event feel so that no matter where it's held, you'll have several features on World Series history," said McCormick, who has worked on the World Series Program for more than a dozen years. "The history is important because that's what the event is all about."

As pages are produced at MLB's Manhattan offices beginning in August, they're sent to Quad Graphics' pre-press plant in New York. Proofs are then sent back to MLB for color correction and approval. The final product is then printed in the Quad Graphics facility in Sussex, Wis., and delivered by truck, or plane if necessary, to the cities hosting the Fall Classic. Cover art is designed for all four possible World Series matchups so that printing can commence as soon as the second League Championship Series ends.

"The program is among the most highly collectible items associated with the event," said Hintze. "Not only does it contain information from some of the most renowned baseball writers of our generation, it's also the perfect keepsake. Many of our fans have programs collected from decades ago and always want to make sure their collection is updated. That's part of what makes the World Series Program so sought after — it's a timeless souvenir."

PARADES

EVERYONE LOVES A parade, especially fans of the World Series champions. For those in charge of planning such celebrations, however, the festivities can present a challenge. In a sport full of superstitious people, nobody wants to jinx a team by preparing for a parade before the victory is sealed. But since the event is usually held the second day after the victory, schedules and routes must be worked out in advance — if ever so quietly.

The victory parade is held soon after the clinching game, before the excitement dies down and players scatter to their offseason homes. The timeliness of the preparation is especially important for the fans of those teams that clinch the championship on the road.

Former Manager Joe Torre's Yankees made the ticker-tape trip through New York's Canyon of Heroes into a near-annual event, traversing the lower Manhattan route four times from 1996 to 2000. The route is one mile long and extends through the Financial District along Broadway from Battery Park to City Hall. It has hosted everyone from Nelson Mandela to Pope John Paul II to the 2008 and 2012 Super Bowl champion New York Giants.

With the celebration parades often snaking around for miles, fans can stake out a good spot or follow the vehicles along. Regardless, the parade gives the team a chance to have fun and revel in the accomplishment while the city gets a close look at its world champions and cheers them on. Cameramen from MLB Productions even ride on floats with players to capture the experience. After their 2006 title, longtime Cardinals Manager Tony La Russa was chosen to lead the parade in a horse-drawn carriage.

The Chicago White Sox and Florida Marlins enjoyed downtown parades when they took home the trophy, but for teams without central downtown areas, building a parade route can require some creativity.

The Angels, who play in Anaheim, held their parade after their victory in 2002 along Main Street in nearby Disneyland. They followed it up with a second one that ended with a celebratory rally in the parking lot at their home field, Angels Stadium.

Then there were the Boston Red Sox, who after winning their first World Series in 86 years in 2004, hosted the biggest parade in Major League Baseball history, drawing an estimated 3 million fans along a seven-mile parade route that even included a leg on the Charles River aboard Duck Tour vehicles.

The day before the celebration, Mayor Thomas Menino added the amphibious leg after Boston police expressed concern that the street route would not provide enough space for spectators. The decision proved to be a wise one given the masses that showed up.

The Phillies' World Series victory in 2008 scuttled initial plans for what would have been the longest parade in World Series history. The Tampa Bay Rays were prepared to travel in a convoy from downtown Tampa over the Gandy Bridge into St. Petersburg and further south to their home stadium, Tropicana Field, a distance of more than 20 miles.

Instead, the Phillies and then 45-year-old pitcher Jamie Moyer got to enjoy a parade. Moyer grew up in Sellersville, Pa., and at the age of 17 attended the team's last World Series parade, in 1980.

"Riding in a World Series parade is something you dream about your whole life," Moyer said. "To see how it brings the city together ... it's an incredible experience."

AT&T PARK

COMMONLY REGARDED AS one of the most picturesque venues in all of sports, AT&T Park has firmly earned a place among the many architectural marvels in the Bay Area, as well as baseball lore. In its 13 seasons of use, it has already hosted five playoff teams, two World Series champions, the 2007 All-Star Game, its franchise's first perfect game and the all-time career home run king.

Located near downtown San Francisco, adjacent to the Bay, fans enter the stadium through a main entrance gate graced by the statue of the greatest Giant of all time, Willie Mays. Once inside, Giants faithful are treated to breathtaking views of the Bay Area, the mouthwatering smell of AT&T Park's signature garlic fries and the sounds of as many as 41,503 Giants faithful singing, dancing and chanting in unison — sometimes in celebration of a rare splash-down home run hit into the brisk waters of McCovey Cove.

Although fans can still get hit with the unmistakable chill of San Francisco on a given day, the stadium fights the elements more effectively than its predecessor down at Candlestick Point. And unlike the Giants' old home, AT&T Park is a baseball stadium through and through. Its brick walls, natural grass playing field and classic, expansive National League dimensions give the stadium a nostalgic yet contemporary feel all its own.

BIRTH OF THE GIANTS

ABOUT 3,000 MILES east of San Francisco and almost 130 years ago, the Giants entered the baseball world as the New York Gothams of the National League. Founded by tobacco mogul John B. Day and player-manager Jim Mutrie, the Gothams enjoyed great success in the 1880s, earning two NL pennants and two victories in the pre-modern World Series.

In 1883, the Giants moved to upper Manhattan and settled into the Polo Grounds. Legend has it that the Gothams became the Giants in 1885, when Mutrie congratulated his team after a particularly convincing victory by calling his players "my big fellows, my giants." The team moved again in 1889, to Coogan's Bluff in Harlem, where they would

remain until they moved to the West Coast in 1957. Unlike the 1880s, the early years in Harlem were not prosperous for the Giants, who underwent three ownership changes before 1902 and did not finish in first place until 1904. But in 1902, in his last impactful decision before he sold the team, Owner Andrew Freedman hired John McGraw. The skipper managed the Giants for three decades, winning three World Series and 10 National League pennants.

After memorable moments in the early 1950s, such as Bobby Thompson's "Shot Heard 'Round The World" and Willie Mays' "Catch," the Giants moved to San Francisco in 1957, thus beginning a new era of Giants baseball that has now seen two World Series champions emerge.

ROSTER

THE 2012 SAN FRANCISCO GIANTS

BRUCE BOCHY
MANAGER

THIS YEAR, THE 57-year-old former Big League catcher became one of 15 managers in history to win more than 1,400 games and multiple World Series. Of Bochy's 1,454 career regular-season victories — good for 23rd on the all-time list — 503 have come with the Giants, whom he has led to four straight seasons of more than 85 wins. His teams have taken on his gritty personality, and he is renowned as one of baseball's best in-game tacticians, especially in handling his bullpen.

COACHING STAFF:
Tim Flannery: Third Base
Mark Gardner: Bullpen
Roberto Kelly: First Base
Hensley Meulens: Hitting
Dave Righetti: Pitching
Ron Wotus: Bench

15

JEREMY AFFELDT
PITCHER

SINCE BEING SIGNED as a free agent in 2008, the 33-year-old southpaw has become a reliable late-inning option out of the bullpen with the ability to shut down both left- and right-handed hitters. His numbers in 2012 — 67 games, 63.1 innings, a 2.70 ERA and a 57:23 strikeout-to-walk ratio — were remarkably consistent with those from 2011 (67, 61.2, 2.63, 54:24). And pressure certainly does not faze Affeldt: He has allowed just two hits and one run in 8.2 career innings in the LCS, including 4.2 scoreless frames against the Cardinals this year.

41

JOAQUIN ARIAS
INFIELD

BEFORE THIS SEASON, Arias' claim to fame was being the "player to be named later" in the trade that sent Alex Rodriguez from the Rangers to the Yankees for Alfonso Soriano. But during his fifth Major League season, the Dominican-born infielder blossomed, playing in a career-high 112 games as primarily a slick-fielding fill-in at short-stop and third base. He swung the bat competently, too, batting .270 with his first five career Big League home runs, before contributing a two-double, two-run effort in Game 4 of the NLDS.

13

BRANDON BELT
FIRST BASE

EXPECTATIONS ARE SKY-HIGH for a player who plowed through the Minor Leagues with a .343 average, 31 home runs and 148 RBI in 189 games. Belt, a fifth-round draft pick in 2010 out of the University of Texas, will be hard-pressed to match those numbers and the fanfare that comes with them at the next level. But in his first full season in the Majors, he found his comfort zone and flashed his All-Star potential as the Giants' regular first baseman. The 6-foot-5 lefty posted an average better than .290 and an OPS better than .875 in three separate months.

9

GREGOR BLANCO
OUTFIELD

IN BUILDING A two-time World Series champion, the Giants have specialized in finding players, like Blanco, who were overlooked by teams throughout the Majors. The 28-year-old thrived this season, playing in more Big League games than he did in the previous three years combined. What he lacked in power hitting he made up for by consistently getting on base (51 walks) and wreaking havoc from there (26 steals). He also provided stability in the outfield by excelling at all three positions, most memorably when he preserved Matt Cain's June 13 perfect game with a diving catch in the seventh that will go down in Giants lore.

7

MADISON BUMGARNER
PITCHER

THERE ARE FEW 23-year-old pitchers as accomplished as Bumgarner. In his second full season with the Giants — following a meteoric rise through the Minors that yielded a 34-6 record and 2.00 ERA — the lefty from Hickory, N.C., posted his second consecutive double-digit win, 200-inning season. He struck out 191 batters for the second straight year while lowering opposing hitters' batting average to .234, eighth-best in the NL. Although he endured a rough patch in September, Bumgarner added seven shutout innings in the World Series and another ring to his growing resume.

EMMANUEL BURRISS
SECOND BASE

ONE OF 18 homegrown players on the 40-man roster, Burriss was the 33rd overall pick in the 2006 draft. He has shuffled between the Majors and Minors over the last five years, contributing speed and the ability to play middle infield off the bench. In 2012, the 27-year-old spent most of his 60 games at second base, while batting .213 with five stolen bases.

MATT CAIN
PITCHER

ON THE SURFACE, Cain's 2012 season wasn't all that much different from the previous three — he again threw more than 215 innings, posted an ERA less than 3.15 and held opponents to a batting average below .235. But make no mistake, this was the Alabama native's crowning season, as he hurled his way into baseball's nationally recognized elite. Throwing a perfect game, as Cain did on June 13, will do that for a pitcher. His perfecto, the first in team history and 22nd all-time, was record-breaking in more ways than one: His 14 strikeouts tied Sandy Koufax for the all-time mark in a perfect game and his 125 pitches set the new standard. He also became the first pitcher to score a run while twirling a perfect game. A month later, Cain started the All-Star Game for the NL and notched the win with two shut-out innings. The 28-year-old's gut-check win in Game 7 of the NLCS added to his reputation as a big-game ace.

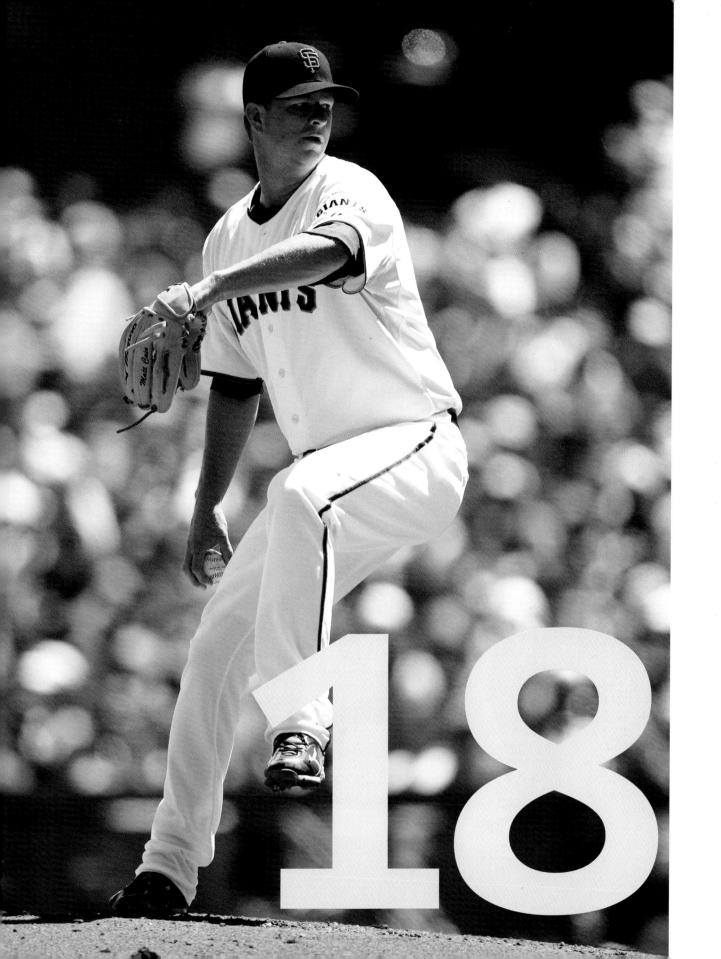

SANTIAGO CASILLA
PITCHER

CASILLA CONTINUES TO be a bonafide steal after signing as a free agent in 2010 and posting an ERA under 2.00 in each of his first two seasons. This year, he took his dominance to the ninth inning, saving 21 games in 23 opportunities during the first three months after Brian Wilson went on the DL. After scuffling in July, he returned to form as a set up man, giving up just five earned runs over his final 28 appearances. In total, he pitched a career-high 63.1 innings and tied his career highs in wins (7) and holds (12).

46

BRANDON CRAWFORD
SHORTSTOP

IN HIS SECOND Big League season, the UCLA product's hitting began to complement his outstanding fielding. Crawford upped his average by 44 points and his OPS by 69 from 2011 to '12, pounding 33 extra-base hits as the Giants' starting shortstop. The improved stroke paid dividends in the do-or-die Game 5 of the NLDS, when his RBI triple kick-started the decisive six-run rally in the fifth inning. And Crawford continued to work magic with his glove, producing highlight-reel plays with regularity.

35

CLAY HENSLEY
PITCHER

HENSLEY RETURNED TO the team that drafted him a decade ago to contribute 50.2 innings out of the bullpen. The right-hander — who was traded to the Padres for reliever Matt Herges in 2003 — shined in the early months of the season, posting a 1.77 ERA through May. His role may have diminished as the season wore on, but Hensley continued to be effective against lefties, holding them to a .241 average.

34

AUBREY HUFF
FIRST BASE

HUFF WAS A hero on the 2010 championship team, slugging 26 homers from the middle of the order. Persistent health problems limited him to just 78 plate appearances in 2012, but his veteran leadership in the clubhouse could still be felt, and he made an impact as a decorated pinch-hitter. The 35-year-old reached base in 13 of his 32 pinch-hit plate appearances for a .406 on-base percentage, including five base-knocks in 16 September appearances.

17

GEORGE KONTOS
PITCHER

IN YET ANOTHER shrewd move, the Giants acquired Kontos for catcher Chris Stewart in April — a trade that proved crucial beginning in June. The 27-year-old had logged more than 550 Minor League innings upon his call-up that month, and his strong numbers (3.24 career ERA) and fastball-slider repertoire translated into Big League success. Kontos' monthly ERAs from June to August were 2.16, 2.25 and 2.20, as he struck out almost exactly one batter per inning overall and compiled a 1.05 WHIP.

70

TIM LINCECUM
PITCHER

THE FREAK'S 2012 campaign was certainly not up to par with any of his previous five. But despite a season-long struggle to rediscover his mechanics and the strike zone, Lincecum pulled it together when his team needed him. He rebounded from a 3-10 first half to go 7-5 after the All-Star break with a more Lincecum-like .243 batting average against. His stuff remained sharp enough to whiff more than a batter per inning and earn him a spot as a long reliever in the postseason. There, the team's 2006 first-round pick recaptured some of his old form, coming through with 4.1 shutdown innings out of the bullpen in Game 4 of the NLDS, as well as making a number of other lights-out appearances in relief to secure the Giants' title run.

55

JAVIER LOPEZ
PITCHER

THE 10-YEAR VETERAN, who was acquired at the 2010 non-waiver trade deadline, continued to thrive as one of the top lefty specialists in the game. Of the 97 left-handed hitters Lopez faced, just 17 got hits, while 22 struck out. The side-arming reliever was at his best following the All-Star break, giving up just two earned runs in 18 innings (1.00 ERA) and even going six for six in save opportunities as a backup closer.

49

JOSE MIJARES
PITCHER

AN AUGUST WAIVER claim, Mijares took his solid stats from Kansas City with him to San Francisco. His ERA and WHIP with the Giants (2.55, 1.25) in his final 17.2 innings were nearly identical to his numbers in his first 38.2 innings with the Royals (2.56, 1.27). The Venezuela native gave the team flexibility out of the bullpen, limiting lefties to a .211 average while being used primarily in the middle innings.

50

GUILLERMO MOTA
PITCHER

AT 39 YEARS OLD, Mota remained effective in his 14th pro season with his seventh different club. He struck out 16 of the 64 righties he faced and, in total, fanned more than a batter per inning for the first time in his career to earn a postseason roster spot. Originally signed by the Mets in 1990 — when many of his teammates were toddlers — Mota also brought a veteran presence to the bullpen, having logged more than 850 Major League innings in his career.

59

XAVIER NADY
OUTFIELD

ACQUIRED IN AUGUST, Nady provided a spark in his very first at-bat in orange and black, hitting a three-run double on Sept. 1 to help his new team to a victory over the Cubs. Nady was productive in his small sample of playing time for San Francisco, hitting for a .733 OPS and providing some much-needed right-handed pop to merit a spot on San Francisco's postseason roster.

12

ANGEL PAGAN
OUTFIELD

ALTHOUGH PAGAN IS not yet an All-Star, he is on the cusp of becoming one. In 2012, he hit 15 triples to lead the Majors and set a San Francisco-era Giants record, while also turning in a 20-game hitting streak and a Giants record 28-game hitting streak at home. By combining prowess at the plate with his exceptional range in center field and a stolen-base success of 29 in 36 attempts, Pagan has proven to be a complete and well-rounded player.

16

HUNTER PENCE
OUTFIELD

ON THE PATH to an improbable championship, Pence became a passionate leader in the Giants' dugout. He earned the nickname "Reverend" from third base coach Tim Flannery in reference to how the club responded to his motivational speeches: by winning the NLDS despite having fallen into an 0-2 hole against the Reds. These pep talks are unusual to baseball, but Pence has a penchant for the unconventional; his broken-bat double in Game 7 of the NLCS hit his bat three times, and the unusual spin and slice of the ball allowed him to break the game open by chasing home three runs.

8

BRAD PENNY
PITCHER

AFTER PITCHING SUCCESSFULLY for the Giants in 2009, Penny returned to San Francisco midway through this season. His track record speaks for itself: He has twice been selected to the All-Star Game, starting the 2006 Midsummer Classic. In 2012, he joined the Giants in late June to log 28 innings out of the bullpen.

31

BRETT PILL
FIRST BASE

PILL HAS SHOWN big-time power throughout his Minor League career, averaging nearly 16 home runs per full season and slamming as many as 25 bombs last year at Triple-A Fresno. In 2011, Pill became the first Giant since Will Clark to hit a home run in his first Major League at-bat, and the next day, he became just the 22nd player in all of baseball since 1919 to hit home runs in each of his first two games.

6

BUSTER POSEY
CATCHER

THE HONORS AND accomplishments that the 25-year-old Posey has been able to collect in just over two full seasons are staggering. In 2010, he helped the Giants win their first championship in San Francisco and was named the NL Rookie of the Year. In 2012, Posey bounced back from injury to earn the nod as the NL's starting catcher in the All-Star Game en route to becoming the MLB batting champion, the NL Comeback Player of the Year and, again, a World Series champ. San Francisco fans serenaded the face of their franchise with "MVP" chants throughout the second half, when Posey hit for a ridiculous 1.102 OPS. A force behind the plate as well as beside it, Posey also threw out the sixth-highest percentage of base stealers in the league and caught Matt Cain's perfect game.

28

SERGIO ROMO
PITCHER

ROMO STEPPED INTO the spotlight this season when he took over the Giants' closing duties in late August, converting nine saves and surrendering no walks in 17.1 innings. In the playoffs, Romo put the finishing touches on five of the Giants' six NLDS and NLCS wins. But despite the increased attention that comes with finishing games, Romo remains underrated. His 14.00 K/BB in 2011 was the third-highest single-season mark since 1900 (with a minimum of 30 innings pitched), and in 2012, he had a spectacular, if not so transcendent, 6.30 K/BB ratio.

54

HECTOR SANCHEZ
CATCHER

WITH SANCHEZ ENTERING the year as one of the Giants' top prospects, many may have thought that his path to the Big Leagues would be hampered by the presence of All-Star catcher Buster Posey. But Sanchez became the backup backstop and saw plenty of time behind the plate when Posey played first base. The 22-year-old held his own with the bat, posting a .280 batting average in 227 plate appearances while burnishing his credentials as a strong thrower, game-caller and receiver.

29

PABLO SANDOVAL
THIRD BASE

THE GIANTS, WHO are lovingly called baseball's band of misfits, are a suitable team for Sandoval, one of the game's most unique players. Since his first full season in 2009, Kung Fu Panda leads active players with the highest percentage of swings at pitches outside the strike zone. But Sandoval's free-swinging ways certainly haven't hampered his success, as he is also one of the best bad-ball hitters in the sport, ranking first in hits and second in home runs on pitches outside the zone. The AT&T Park crowds don panda heads and hats in reverence to their third baseman, who is known for his exuberance and knack for the big hit. This was exemplified by his performance in Game 1 of the Fall Classic, when he joined Babe Ruth, Reggie Jackson and Albert Pujols as the only players to ever hit three homers in one World Series game.

MARCO SCUTARO
SECOND BASE

FOR YEARS, SCUTARO was one of MLB's best super-subs, an infielder with great plate discipline who has since evolved into a solid starter. When the Giants traded for the second baseman at the deadline, Scutaro had his first chance for major postseason playing time since 2006, an opportunity that he seized and sprinted away with. He earned NLCS MVP honors, tying a record with 14 hits while playing scintillating defense and, fittingly, catching the final out through the raindrops to seal San Francisco's trip to the Fall Classic.

19

RYAN THERIOT
SECOND BASE

THERIOT HAD A solid NLCS this year, helping topple the reigning champs — his former club — with RBI hits that placed Giants leads further out of St. Louis' reach. He entered Game 2 in place of Marco Scutaro and hit a two-run single to put the score at 7-1, and in Game 6, he gave San Francisco a commanding 6-1 lead with a two-out run-scoring single. This is his second straight World Series championship.

5

RYAN VOGELSONG
PITCHER

DURING THE MID-2000s, Vogelsong was a journeyman if there ever was one, spending years moving from stop to stop in the Minor Leagues and even Japan at one point. Now, he's firmly entrenched in the Giants' rotation as one of the most dependable No. 3 starters in the league. In two years, he has won 27 games on the strength of his 3.05 ERA, earned an All-Star nod in 2011 and outdueled Chris Carpenter twice in the 2012 NLCS.

32

BRIAN WILSON
PITCHER

WHEN WILSON WENT down early this season with Tommy John surgery, many wondered how the team would replace him. The fact that the Giants filled in for their superstar closer with another unhittable (and black-bearded) fireman in Sergio Romo speaks to the team's resilience and great bullpen depth. But Wilson remained a commanding presence in the dugout, intensely supporting his teammates while keeping things loose with his eccentric behavior.

38

BARRY ZITO
PITCHER

ZITO TURNED IN what may have been his best season as a Giant, pitching to a 4.15 ERA across 184.1 innings. It started with a bang, as Zito threw a complete-game shutout in his first start of the season against Colorado, but for Giants fans, the enduring image of his 2012 season will be one of his last starts. With the Giants down 3-1 in the NLCS, they called Zito to the hill, and he was flawless. He tossed 7.2 scoreless innings and struck out six to stave off elimination and send the series back to San Francisco for Games 6 and 7. It turned the tide against the Cardinals, and the Giants rode that wave of momentum all the way to their seventh world championship.

75

2012 SEASON IN REVIEW

BASEBALL IS A game of months and moments, drawn-out dramas and once-in-a-lifetime plays. In 2012, the game was shaped by both season-long storylines — the farewell tour of an aging hero, a steadily developing quest to capture the Triple Crown and the appearance of a powerhouse in the nation's capital 79 years after the District boasted its last playoff contender — and record-breaking moments, including hits, homers and strikeouts that vaulted their owners to new plateaus and new levels of stardom.

In between, games everywhere from nine to 19 innings long contained their own tales of tragedy and triumph. Pitchers in search of perfection — or the fountain of youth — devastated hitters, while other sluggers hoisted bats in Herculean displays of strength and skill.

Down the stretch, an extra playoff spot made many games must-see TV. Catch up on any of the action you missed during the season right here.

BEST OF 2012

PITCHING RICHES

TOP-NOTCH PERFORMANCES on the mound started early this year, with Philip Humber twirling a perfect game on April 21 for Chicago. Less than two weeks later, Jered Weaver of the Angels held the Twins hitless. On June 1, two-time Cy Young Award winner Johan Santana threw the first no-hitter in Mets history. The most unconventional no-no came a week later, when six Seattle pitchers combined to blank the Dodgers after starter Kevin Millwood was pulled from the game with an injury. And on Sept. 28, the Reds' Homer Bailey threw the seventh no-no of the season, tying the modern record.

Even among all the gems this season, Matt Cain's perfect game on June 13 stood out with his career-high 14 strikeouts, tying Sandy Koufax's record for the most K's in a perfect game. Cain was also the first pitcher to score a run during his perfect game. On Aug. 15, Seattle's King Felix Hernandez helped set a new record for perfect games in a season with the third of the year.

FINAL STANDINGS

AMERICAN LEAGUE

East	W	L	GB
xNew York	95	67	-
yBaltimore	93	69	2
Tampa Bay	90	72	5
Toronto	73	89	22
Boston	69	93	26

Central	W	L	GB
xDetroit	88	74	-
Chicago	85	77	3
Kansas City	72	90	16
Cleveland	68	94	20
Minnesota	66	96	22

West	W	L	GB
xOakland	94	68	-
yTexas	93	69	1
Los Angeles	89	73	5
Seattle	75	87	19

x Division winner; y Wild Card

NATIONAL LEAGUE

East	W	L	GB
xWashington	98	64	-
yAtlanta	94	68	4
Philadelphia	81	81	17
New York	74	88	24
Miami	69	93	29

Central	W	L	GB
xCincinnati	97	65	-
ySt. Louis	88	74	9
Milwaukee	83	79	14
Pittsburgh	79	83	18
Chicago	61	101	36
Houston	55	107	42

West	W	L	GB
xSan Francisco	94	68	-
Los Angeles	86	76	8
Arizona	81	81	13
San Diego	76	86	18
Colorado	64	98	30

2012 CATEGORY LEADERS

AMERICAN LEAGUE

Batting Average	Miguel Cabrera, Detroit	.330
Hits	Derek Jeter, New York	216
Home Runs	Miguel Cabrera, Detroit	44
RBI	Miguel Cabrera, Detroit	139
Stolen Bases	Mike Trout, Los Angeles	49
Wins	David Price, Tampa Bay	20
	Jered Weaver, Los Angeles	
ERA	David Price, Tampa Bay	2.56
Strikeouts	Justin Verlander, Detroit	239
Saves	Jim Johnson, Baltimore	51

NATIONAL LEAGUE

Batting Average	Buster Posey, San Francisco	.336
Hits	Andrew McCutchen, Pittsburgh	194
Home Runs	Ryan Braun, Milwaukee	41
RBI	Chase Headley, San Diego	115
Stolen Bases	Everth Cabrera, San Diego	44
Wins	Gio Gonzalez, Washington	21
ERA	Clayton Kershaw, Los Angeles	2.53
Strikeouts	R.A. Dickey, New York	230
Saves	Craig Kimbrel, Atlanta	42
	Jason Motte, St. Louis	

133

APRIL 2012

AUSPICIOUS BEGINNINGS

Through the season's first two weeks, **Matt Kemp** hit .481 with eight home runs to lead the Dodgers to their best season-opening 10-game record since 1981 at 9-1. Kemp went on to break the club record for home runs in April, hitting his 11th for a walk-off win against the Nationals on April 28.

WE ARE YOUNG

Could former Arizona Fall League teammates Mike Trout and Bryce Harper have foreseen their parallel success? On April 28, the then-20-year-old Trout returned to the Bigs after two stints in 2011 and sparked the Angels. The same day, Harper made his debut at 19 years old for the Nationals. The two re-sumed their friendship at the All-Star Game.

OLD TIME'S SAKE

Two hundred players and coaches from throughout Red Sox history turned out to celebrate Fenway Park's centennial on April 20 in front of the 719th consecutive sellout crowd. Current players in throwback uniforms joined fan favorites from Johnny Pesky to Terry Francona on the field before taking on the Yankees — the same opponent the team faced 100 years before.

AFTER MISSING OUT on the playoffs entirely in 2011, the Giants got off to a rough start in 2012, getting swept by the Diamondbacks in their first three-game series. In the fourth game of the season, they notched their first win behind the man left off the postseason roster when the team won the World Series two years before, Barry Zito, who pitched his first complete-game shutout in a Giants uniform for a 7-0 win over the Rockies on April 9.

Four days later, perennial ace Matt Cain flirted with perfection — a sign of things to come — against the Pirates, giving up just one hit and no walks in a 5-0 victory. In the bullpen, three-time All-Star Brian Wilson's season-ending Tommy John surgery — after he appeared in just two games — left the closer's spot open for the first time since 2008. The task fell to a rotating cast of relievers, with right-hander Santiago Casilla getting the first shot and converting all four of his save opportunities in the first month.

Pablo Sandoval powered the offense, roaring out of the gate to put together a new franchise-record hitting streak to start a season. The sweet-swinging third baseman recorded a hit in his first 20 games, giving him a .311 average for the month and pushing the Giants to two games over .500 by the end of April.

MAY 2012

MUSCLE MAN

On May 21, Marlins outfielder **Giancarlo Stanton** proved too much for the soft-tossing Jamie Moyer and the brand-new Marlins Park to contain. He smashed a grand slam an estimated 438 feet — directly into the scoreboard, which suffered a temporary blackout of several panels.

POWER PLAY

Prior to May 13, Reds slugger **Joey Votto** was hitting for average (.296) but not power, with just two longballs on the season. But that changed in a single game when he more than doubled his home run count, going 4 for 5 with three homers — including a walk-off grand slam to carry his club to a 9-6 win over the Nationals.

FOUR FOR THE BOOKS

Texas Rangers star **Josh Hamilton** made history on May 8 when he became just the 16th player to hit four home runs in one game to give Texas a 10-3 victory over Baltimore. The 2010 AL MVP set another record later in the season when he amassed more votes than any player in MLB history to garner his fifth consecutive All-Star Game selection.

NOT TO BE outdone, **Angel Pagan** put together a 20-game hitting streak that ended on May 7, which gave him and teammate Pablo Sandoval the longest streaks in the Majors to that point. During that stretch, Pagan, an offseason acquisition, was 28 for 89 with nine extra-base hits, seven RBI and 11 runs scored, although the team managed just a 10-10 record. He remained hot all month, ending May with a .375 average. In a 14-7 rout of the Miami Marlins on the 24th, Pagan was responsible for four RBI, including a bases-loaded double to break a tie, backing 6.1 strong innings by Ryan Vogelsong.

After spending years in relative obscurity, the 35-year-old journeyman pitcher stayed on pace with his 2011 All-Star season in 2012. He won three of his four decisions in six May starts, giving up just 33 hits in 41.2 innings pitched. His best outing came in the form of seven one-hit, shutout innings on the 19th in a 4-0 win against the A's that secured his ERA for the month at an impressive 1.51. And even without their bearded leader, the bullpen became a force to be reckoned with, en route to compiling the second-most saves in the league on the season.

In May, most of that burden was shouldered by 32-year-old Dominican righty Casilla, who closed out 10 games in the month with an ERA of 1.26 and a 4:1 strikeout-to-walk ratio. Despite failing to put together a sweep at any point in the month, the Giants went 15-14 in May to end the month 5.5 games out of first in the NL West.

JUNE 2012

TWICE IN A BLUE MOON

Before this year, just three players in MLB history had hit for the cycle twice in a season. The last hitter to accomplish the feat was Babe Herman in 1931. Then, on June 18 and 29, Diamondbacks second baseman **Aaron Hill** did it twice — in just one month.

ONE SHORT OF NONE

Even in such a pitching-rich era, **R.A. Dickey** stands out. Since reinventing himself as a knuckleballer, the 37-year-old has evolved into a dominant force on the mound. On June 18, he threw his second consecutive one-hitter, notching a personal best 13 strikeouts. Dickey finished his first All-Star season with an impressive 20 wins and a 2.73 ERA, both second in the NL.

THE 300 CLUB

When he stole his 300th base on June 15, Cardinals outfielder **Carlos Beltran** not only joined an elite club that put him in the ranks of Barry Bonds and Willie Mays with 300 stolen bases and 300-plus home runs, he also started his own club: switch-hitters to accomplish the feat.

WHAT ELSE COULD possibly steal the spotlight in the Giants' June except **Matt Cain**'s perfect game on the 13th? It was more than just the 22nd perfecto in Big League history. In front of a fired up crowd at AT&T Park, cheering like it was the last out of the World Series on every strike in the late innings, Cain became the first Giants pitcher to achieve perfection, and his 14 K's on the night were matched only by Sandy Koufax for the most in a perfect game. The 28-year-old three-time All-Star also became the first pitcher ever to score a run while pitching a perfect game, as one of 10 Giants to cross the plate in the win over Houston.

But in a 17-11 June that saw the Giants ascend to the top of the NL West for the first time all season, Cain was hardly the only San Francisco pitcher to stymie the opposition. From June 25–28, the Giants strung together 36 consecutive scoreless innings, a new team record since moving to San Francisco in 1958. The lights-out streak was capped off by 23-year-old Madison Bumgarner's first career shutout. The tall lefty achieved a notable feat on his own earlier in the month when he hit the first home run of his career in the same game that he also recorded 12 strikeouts, becoming just the fifth pitcher in the past three decades to do so.

JULY 2012

NATIONAL OFFENSE

In the 83rd annual Midsummer Classic, the National League took the lead early with a five-run first and never looked back. Recently retired skipper **Tony La Russa** was back at the helm for the 8-0 win, which earned the NL home-field advantage in the World Series for the third straight year.

PRINCE CROWNED

Prince Fielder became just the second slugger to capture the Home Run Derby trophy multiple times, winning his second title on July 9 at Kansas City's Kauffman Stadium. His dozen blasts in the final round bested the Blue Jays' Jose Bautista.

CLUTCH 'CUTCH

In the first half of the season, the Pirates were a force to be reckoned with thanks to their speedy center fielder, **Andrew Mc-Cutchen**. The two-time All-Star's most impressive offensive display came in July, when he hit .446 with seven home runs and 15 RBI, leading the Bucs to a stellar 17-9 record that month.

THREE MONTHS BEFORE the Giants clinched a World Series berth, four members of the team helped secure home-field advantage in the Fall Classic as part of the winning National League team in the All-Star Game. Cain proved to be the best of the best on the mound, capturing the win in the 8-0 rout by the Senior Circuit. Team-mate Melky Cabrera won the MVP Award while Sandoval kick-started the NL offense with a bases-loaded triple off Tigers ace Justin Verlander in the first inning.

Buster Posey also earned a starting spot in Kansas City for his strong opening months of the season, but it was nothing compared to his second half. In the final three months of the season, Posey added nearly 100 points to his average to capture the batting title, due in large part to an incredible .381 clip in July. The young catcher contributed an impressive 21 RBI in the month, four of which came during a 7-1 victory over San Diego on the 23rd.

As the non-waiver trade deadline approached, the Giants made moves to bolster their offense. From the Phillies came two-time All-Star outfielder Hunter Pence and from the Rockies came 36-year-old veteran Marco Scutaro. A sweep at the hands of the second-place Dodgers at the end of the month left the Giants just one game ahead of their NL West rivals as the calendar turned to August.

AUGUST 2012

MR. CONSISTENCY

On Aug. 11, **Derek Jeter** hit a ground-rule double that bounced over the right-field wall. In a career that already included more than 3,000 hits, the sixth-inning knock hardly seemed a cause for celebration. But with it, the 13-time All-Star achieved a distinction previously held exclusively by Hank Aaron: reaching 150 or more hits in 17 consecutive seasons.

LIFETIME ACHIEVEMENTS

Hulking power hitter **Adam Dunn** smashed through two milestones during his bounce-back season. On Aug. 13, the White Sox first baseman recorded his 1,000th career RBI against Toronto. Five days later, in the eighth inning of a loss to the Royals, he became the 50th MLB player to reach 400 career home runs.

THE MIDSEASON ACQUISITIONS wasted no time before putting their bats to work for the Giants. Pence and **Marco Scutaro**, along with nearly all of their new teammates, contributed to a 15-0 rout over the defending champion Cardinals on Aug. 8. The NL East import had two RBI singles on the night. But it was Scutaro who really made his presence felt with seven RBI — the most by any Giants player in more than a decade — including a ninth-inning grand slam. Vogelsong earned the win for his seven shutout innings, bringing his season record up to 10-5. Fellow starters Cain and Bumgarner remained consistent on the mound, with each posting an August ERA lower than 3.00. And the bullpen was simply dominant: Late-inning options Casilla, Romo and lefty Javier Lopez each kept their ERA under 1.00, while George Kontos shined in the middle innings.

The Giants' offense also got a boost from an unexpected source in August, as utility infielder Joaquin Arias had a banner month, batting .417 with a .717 slugging percentage in 24 games. On Aug. 22 he recorded a career-high five RBI to give the Giants an 8-4 victory over the Dodgers. The win capped a three-game sweep of San Francisco's division rivals, and gave the club an inch of breathing room with a 2.5-game lead in the NL West. A sweep of the Astros in the final week of August put the Giants a more comfortable 4.5 games up heading into the final full month.

143

SEPTEMBER 2012

NATIONAL PASTIME

In the nation's capital, the final game saw a team that had led the league throughout the season secure home-field advantage in its first year of postseason participation. The Nationals' 5-1 victory gave Washington a Major League–leading 98 wins two days after clinching the NL East. This year marked the District's first playoff berth since the Senators lost the 1933 World Series. In their eighth year in the country's capital, the Nationals toppled traditional powerhouses in the NL East behind the dynamic performances of young players like Stephen Strasburg, Bryce Harper and Gio Gonzalez.

A-PLUS

Fortunately for the Oakland A's, baseball's regular season isn't over until the final out of the 162nd game. And when closer **Grant Balfour** set down the final Rangers hitter on Oct. 3, the A's secured their 15th division title in the city's history, and first since 2006. It was the only time all season that Oakland held sole possession of first place. The team overcame an early four-run deficit to win the decisive game, 12-5 — a fitting end for the first team in history to claim the division title after trailing by five games with less than 10 to play.

But overcoming that challenge was just one part of their surge to baseball's best record in the final four months of the season (72-39). After trailing Texas most of the year, Oakland faced off against its division rivals in the final three games, and earned its place in the LDS with a dramatic sweep.

Celebrating with the team when it first clinched a playoff berth two days earlier was pitcher Brandon McCarthy, in the midst of a speedy recovery after being struck in the head by a line drive a month before.

WITH EXACTLY 30 games left in the regular season, the Giants played their best baseball in September and into October, going 20-10 down the stretch. Not content with a single game of offensive brilliance, future NLCS MVP Scutaro posted an astronomical .402 batting average during that time, rounding out a .362 clip in his 61 games after joining the Giants.

Over the course of the season, the Giants led baseball in triples, a testament to their versatile offense and bold baserunning. And first among his speedy teammates was Pagan, who set a San Francisco–era team record for three-baggers with his 13th on Sept. 15. Less than a week later, he legged out his career-high and Major League–leading 15th triple. The middle-of-the-order bats behind Pagan also produced in big ways. Sandoval hit four home runs — his most in a month since April — and recorded 18 RBI, while Posey posted a .371 average and Pence drove in 23 runs.

The following day, on Sept. 22, the Giants clinched their second NL West title in three years with an 8-4 victory over the Padres. Late-season closer **Sergio Romo** was on the mound for the final out, a fitting end to a month that saw the reliever convert six saves while surrendering no walks and posting a paltry 1.23 ERA. Even after snagging a spot in the playoffs, the Giants continued to shape the postseason landscape that awaited them in October, ending the Dodgers' playoff hopes with a victory over Los Angeles on the second to last day of the season.

TRIPLE CROWN

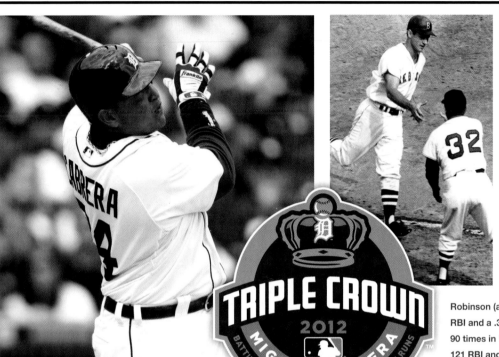

Robinson (above right) posted 49 homers, 122 RBI and a .316 average while striking out just 90 times in '66. Yaz (center) had 44 homers, 121 RBI and a .326 average with a mere 69 strikeouts in '67. This year, Cabrera also kept his K's below 100 en route to the Crown.

ACROSS THE BOARD

Even before whispers around baseball started to circulate that this might finally be the year to witness one of the game's rarest feats, **Miguel Cabrera** had the makings of a Triple Crown winner. In 2008, Cabrera's first year with the Detroit Tigers, the then-25-year-old led the league in home runs with 37. Two years later, he led the league in RBI with 126. The year after that, he took home the batting title with a .344 average. And it wasn't for lack of consistency that the honor evaded the Venezuela-born third baseman. Since his first full Major League season in 2004, Cabrera has hit for a .321 batting average with 34 homers and 118 RBI per season. This season, the right-handed slugger put it all together, leading the American League with a .330 average, 44 home runs and 139 RBI to capture the Triple Crown.

In the age of acronym-heavy stats and *Moneyball* mentality, many have wondered if the Triple Crown is a relic from a different era in baseball. But as decade after decade passed without a winner, the aura surrounding the achievement grew. Prior to Cabrera, just 11 players had achieved the mark since 1900. Jimmie Foxx and Lou Gehrig won it back-to-back in 1933 and '34. Frank Robinson won in 1966, and the following year Carl Yastrzemski sparked a revival in Boston by bringing home the honor. Since then, Hall of Famers and MVPs have come close, but no one has succeeded. But the 45-year drought is indicative not of a decrease in star power, but rather of a more competitive field throughout baseball. Indeed, consider this: Even if he went head-to-head with Yastrzemski in his best season, Cabrera would still have won the Triple Crown this year.

"Miguel was outstanding all year long by coming to play every day, showing his discipline at the plate and making the most of his great talent," Robinson, now MLB's executive vice president for baseball development, said in October. "Most importantly, Miguel and the Tigers had the opportunity to participate in the most exciting month of the baseball season."

.330 BA
44 HR
139 RBI

Wilson struck out Nelson Cruz for the final out of the 2010 World Series. The eccentric closer saved six games during the playoff run.

WHAT A RELIEF

After years of torture, the San Francisco Giants rode a baseball arm-ageddon to the top in 2010.

THE FIRST THING to know about the Giants franchise, entering the 2010 postseason and dating back to its years in New York, is that it had more representatives in Cooperstown than any other Big League club. Normally, any rank of accumulated glory in baseball includes the conditional "other than the Yankees," as in, "No team — other than the Yankees — has won more AL pennants than the Athletics." Yet 55 Giants players can be found on Hall of Fame plaques — nine more than the Dodgers and, for good measure, 12 more than those very same New York Yankees.

The second item is far less pleasant. Somehow, in the 52 years since the club moved from New York, the Giants had managed to win all of zero championships. In fact, not since 1954, when Hall of Famer Willie Mays raced back to rob Vic Wertz at the Polo Grounds and gave baseball writers a metaphor for the next century or so, had the Giants managed to add to their collection of world titles, a number that stood at five entering 2010.

The first few years of Tim Lincecum's career were truly awesome, but it was a reach to peg him for the Hall of Fame so early. In fact, if their careers all ended that season, not a single member of the 2010 Giants would likely add to the franchise's roster in Cooperstown. Conversely, you could make a reasonable argument that somewhere between four and six members of the 2009 Yankees likely were on the Hall-of-Fame track the minute Game 6 of that Fall Classic ended.

THE 2010 PLAYOFFS began in a way befitting the six months they followed. On day one of the postseason, Philadelphia's Roy Halladay held the Reds' powerful offense hitless. The Year of the Pitcher was extending into October.

The next day, Lincecum began the Giants' series against the Braves by going the full nine and allowing just two hits and a walk against his 14 strikeouts. Doc's no-no had the baseball world enrapt, but Bill James' "game score" metric actually rated Lincecum's effort higher. The start was both memorable and appropriate. Flash and substance aside, you overlooked the Giants' pitching staff at your own peril.

On paper, San Francisco's offense was about as scary as Casper the Friendly Ghost. But the pitching rotation was like Room 217 in *The Shining*. "To get here," the Rangers' Michael Young said before the Series, "you need to have great pitching. The Giants have that. All their starters have been great."

Lincecum owns the 2008 and '09 NL Cy Young Awards. In 2010, Matt Cain was the perfect No. 2 — quiet and steady, and deadly on the mound. Jonathan Sanchez was as good as any pitcher on the days he was good. Madison Bumgarner was yet another young future star (because

Infielder Juan Uribe, who lifted the Giants by hitting two clutch postseason home runs, celebrated with his teammates.

Cain came up big for the 2010 champions, giving up no earned runs in all three of his postseason starts.

the Giants didn't have enough of those…). Barry Zito might not have been the same pitcher from his 2002 Cy Young season, but go find a much better fifth starter.

And that was just the rotation. Throw in bullpen arms like Brian Wilson and Sergio Romo, and you start to see how the Rangers' offense could have been held to a .190 average and just three homers in five games. "What they're doing, they showed all season long and through the playoffs," Romo said of the starters after Game 5. "One through five were solid. For me, it's an honor that I was able to pitch alongside these guys."

For that, Romo can thank GM Brian Sabean and Dick Tidrow, the club's VP of player personnel. Tidrow oversaw the drafts that landed Cain (2002), Wilson (2003), Sanchez (2004), Romo (2005), Lincecum (2006), Bumgarner (2007) and 2010 NL Rookie of the Year Buster Posey (2008). "We have a pretty good scouting eye," Sabean told *Sports Illustrated* during the Series, "and through development our pitching has become the gold standard and the foundation of the organization."

That October, everything began with Lincecum, the 5-foot-11 (yeah, right) toothpick with the crazy delivery. He won Game 1 in all three of the Giants' series, beating Halladay in the NLCS and Cliff Lee in the World Series.

"That's who we want out there," Cain said before the Series. "He doesn't have the typical build of a pitcher, but

is using his talent to the max and finding ways to get it done. Hopefully, it inspires kids who don't have the typical body type."

Cain followed with 7.2 shutout innings in Game 2 (he didn't give up a single earned run in 21.1 postseason frames), and Bumgarner gave a rookie effort for the ages in Game 4, going eight shutout innings and allowing just three hits to become the fourth youngest pitcher to win a Series game.

In the same way people had been counting out the Giants all year, nobody believed the young rotation — with all four 27 or younger — could dominate offenses like those in Philly and Texas come October. Instead, the rotation rolled out a performance that would have impressed the dominant Orioles staff of the late '60s and early '70s, recording a 2.38 ERA on the sport's biggest stage. During Game 4, sportswriter Jeff Fletcher sent out a perfect sarcastic tweet: "Isn't it weird how the Giants have run into another team not swinging the bat well? Just like the Phillies … and Braves."

IN THE GIANTS' clubhouse, Cain is the elder statesman, of sorts. The longest-tenured member of the team, Cain saw the entire 2010 championship club develop, transitioning from the Barry Bonds/Felipe Alou era to the champagne toasts and parades of that November.

Lincecum won Game 1 in all three of the Giants' playoff series in 2010, posting a 2.43 ERA and 43 strike-outs to just nine walks overall.

Edgar Renteria (above) acknowledged the crowd during the team's victory parade. The shortstop smacked the game-winning homer in the seventh inning of the Game 5 clincher. Ian Kinsler (below) missed a golden opportunity in Game 1, grounding into a double play with the bases loaded in the first.

Cain was 26 years old, by the way. "We've always felt like we had a good group of guys over here ever since I've been here," he said before Game 1. That might be the case. But there's no doubting the work that GM Brian Sabean and Co. did plucking from the league's discard pile over the past few years.

Pat Burrell may have suffered through a brutal World Series, striking out 11 times and putting just two balls in play. But after the team picked him up that May, he contributed 18 homers and an .872 OPS to the Giants' postseason run, boosting the club's anemic offense.

Javier Lopez was phenomenal out of the bullpen as a left-handed specialist, neutralizing the Phillies' biggest strength and giving Giants Manager Bruce Bochy a weapon to use against the Rangers' left-handed hitters like Josh Hamilton.

Then there was Cody Ross. Picked up off the waiver wire on Aug. 22, Ross became a San Fran folk hero on par with Jerry Garcia.

It began in Game 1 of the NLCS, a Tim Lincecum–Roy Halladay matchup for the ages. Halladay was coming off his no-hitter, and breezed through the first 2.1 innings before Ross came to bat. His homer to left-center was the first hit and first run that Halladay had allowed in his postseason career. And Ross wasn't done. Two innings later, with the game tied, 1-1, he again came to the plate with one out and placed the ball in almost the exact same spot, a couple of rows beyond Citizens Bank Park's left-center-field wall. He'd go on to win NLCS MVP honors, batting .350 with another home run thrown in. If anyone best represented the Giants' castoffs-and-misfits persona, it was the New Mexico native who used to dream of becoming a rodeo clown.

"I didn't think it was going to be a big deal when I did it," the ever-smiling Ross said of his two-homer game off Halladay. "I was like, 'I've done that before. I've hit two homers in a game before. It's not that big of a deal.'

"But it's been amazing. I can't think of words to describe how it's been. It's something that you dream of and that you hope for as a kid, and we're finally living it."

"This team is a cast of characters," said former Giant J.T. Snow, now a special assistant to the club. "The neatest thing for them is that nobody outside of this clubhouse thought that they could get it done." ◆

At the Helm

AS A HALLOWEEN joke during the 2010 Series, a young Texas fan shaved his head to dress up as Rangers Manager Ron Washington, a hilarious look for a 9-year-old. How could one assemble a costume of Giants Manager Bruce Bochy? "Well, he'd have to blow his head up somehow," Bochy said before Game 5.

It's true, Bochy has a large head — his hat is the biggest in the Majors. But whatever he's got under that size 8-plus cap worked just fine in 2010. His offensively challenged team scored 29 runs in the five Series games. His young mound staff threw lights out. He shook up the lineup almost nightly. "What makes a good manager?" Bochy said during the travel day between Games 2 and 3. "Good players. There's no getting around that. But hopefully, you're doing something to help them by being prepared, being in the right frame of mind to have some success."

Bochy's a baseball lifer who played parts of nine seasons in the Bigs prior to becoming a coach. He managed the Padres for 12 years, winning Manager of the Year in 1996 and the NL pennant in 1998. But, at last, he took the biggest prize in 2010. "If it wasn't for him, we wouldn't be here," outfielder Cody Ross said after Game 5. "He made great call after great call. He's been doing it for a long time and he's one of the winningest managers in the league. He's fun to play for, that's for sure."

The Giants' trade for Scutaro
four days before the deadline
turned out to be monumental.

THE NEW DEAL

This summer, some teams decided not to play the hands they were dealt.
Instead, they made moves and took risks based on the changed postseason format.

NINE-PLUS GAMES back of any shot at the postseason might have seemed like too tall of a hill to climb in seasons past. Not impossible, for sure — as baseball fans learned last year when the Cardinals maneuvered their way past a 10.5-game August deficit in the NL Wild Card race to secure not just a place in the playoffs, but the World Series title — but certainly a formidable obstacle. But nine-plus games out of the last Wild Card spot is exactly where eight National League teams stood on July 31, the day of Major League Baseball's official non-waiver trade deadline.

As it turns out, that's where most of those teams remained more than a month later, when the repercussions of the deadline-beating moves made in the days before the calendar turned to August could be felt throughout the league. Except this year, an additional club received a berth into the playoffs. The prospect of making it to the dance loomed for a host of teams whose seasons would have previously been sealed. "It gives all teams across the league a better chance to get in," says Baltimore Orioles closer Jim Johnson of the new format.

Aside from some flip-flopping at the lower end of the spectrum, the Senior Circuit's standings didn't look all that different on Sept. 1 than they did on July 31. The leaders — Washington, Cincinnati and San Francisco — were still the leaders.

The American League, however, presented a less clear picture. From the vantage point of that last day in July, more teams than ever before appeared to have a shot at October, with just two clubs a seemingly insurmountable

12-plus games out of Wild Card contention. With less than 30 games to go, the division leaders — New York, Chicago and Texas — again remained the same. But where the gap had widened for some, it had closed for others, leaving eight postseason contenders vying for five highly coveted playoff spots.

"You see a lot of teams with similar records," Toronto slugger Jose Bautista said midseason, "and that's good for the game, and brings it to a different level when everybody's got a chance. In the last couple of years the game has been at one of the most competitive levels, and you see it every single day when you step out on the diamond."

But just how much were the league's standings affected by what happened between late July and the end of the regular season? Trades were made, lineups were stacked and rotations were bolstered, and the reinforcements arrived. Just how much did the new postseason format, which was finalized in early March and added a second Wild Card spot for each league, truly shake things up? After all, it simply guarantees a one-game opportunity — essentially a play-in game — that still requires clubs to have what it takes to outlast the competition in October.

"It's going to be very interesting to see how the trade market plays out," Baltimore Orioles General Manager Dan Duquette said earlier this season. "We do know that having another opportunity to make the playoffs will give fans and teams in several cities hope that they can advance to the big dance. But what the market will be, it's difficult to say."

Rodriguez went 5-4 with a 3.72 ERA in 12 starts for the Pirates after being dealt from Houston, where he had spent his first seven seasons.

IN RETROSPECT, WE *can* say how the market played out in the weeks leading up to and immediately following the trade deadline. Sellers certainly weren't shy about unloading some big names in exchange for prospects to help them rebuild for future contention. And while few clubs on the fringe made major moves to improve their chances of contending this year, buyers could be found near the top of each division's standings, shoring up their chances for immediate World Series triumph. The sellers, it seemed, had the leverage, as non-contending teams were able to dump excess salary onto those willing to swallow large contracts for the sake of a trophy.

Despite all the statistical evidence against them, the Orioles managed to make some small plays to keep the pressure on their AL East rivals. Jim Thome came over from Philadelphia on June 30, providing a power bat until being sidelined with nagging injuries. But he rejoined the team in late September, just in time to make a playoff push. Duquette also scooped up utility infielder Omar Quintanilla from the Mets on July 20, acquired southpaw

Joe Saunders from the D-backs in late August and picked up Randy Wolf after he was released by Milwaukee for some relief work — albeit a short-lived stint, as Wolf's season ended prematurely due to a torn elbow ligament.

"People talk about how tough the AL East is, and when you have the quality that we have in our division, to win the Wild Card — just to get in — takes a lot of work," Johnson said. "We've gone through ups and downs this year, but we've proven that we could compete. Obviously having that extra Wild Card helped us."

The perennial AL East powerhouse in the Bronx didn't shy away from wheeling and dealing this summer, either, despite boasting an AL-leading 60-43 record at the trade deadline. With an injured Brett Gardner in a limited role, New York sprang a surprise trade for Mariners hit man Ichiro Suzuki a week before the deadline, adding the speedy veteran outfielder to the lineup for some instant gratification at the price of two Minor Leaguers. And with veteran Alex Rodriguez sidelined with a broken hand, Yankees GM Brian Cashman also picked up Casey McGehee from Pittsburgh to man the hot corner until A-Rod's return.

The Pirates didn't recoup much for McGehee by netting reliever Chad Qualls, but they did pick up some pieces elsewhere in 24-year-old outfielder Travis Snider from Toronto and first baseman Gaby Sanchez, who left behind a Marlins team that defied most preseason projections by lagging far behind in the standings by midsummer. Starter Wandy Rodriguez was arguably Pittsburgh's biggest import, as the Astros loaded up on a trio of prospects in exchange for the left-hander. Rodriguez improved his ERA in his first nine outings with his new NL Central club, and his other stats remained consistent enough for him to solidify the Bucs' rotation for the stretch run.

"It's nice to have the two Wild Cards, but we're not trying to go for a Wild Card," Pirates closer Joel Hanrahan said early this season. "You want to win your division. If you win a Wild Card, you still have one game to go. That one game is a big game. It'd be nice to be able to sit at home in Pittsburgh and watch that game on TV, you know? But it made things a little more interesting this year."

THINGS CERTAINLY GOT interesting across the state in Philadelphia, where the team that won the NL East for the last five seasons suddenly found itself burdened by both injuries and contracts it no longer wanted to hold onto. So, on the same July day, Phillies GM Ruben Amaro Jr. unloaded Hunter Pence, whom the team had acquired

The Giants had a one-game lead in the NL West when they acquired Pence on July 31; they went on to win their division by eight games.

After coming over to the Giants midseason, Pence quickly emerged as one of the club's most respected leaders.

at last year's deadline, to the Giants and shipped Shane Victorino, in the final year of his contract, to Los Angeles.

But the surprises didn't stop there, as the non-waiver trade deadline doesn't prevent late-season deals from being made. Any player who has been placed on and clears waivers after July 31 can be dealt, something Adrian Gonzalez experienced on Aug. 25 when he and teammates Josh Beckett, Carl Crawford and Nick Punto wound up being introduced as members of the Dodgers. Los Angeles agreed to add Beckett, Punto and an out-of-commission Crawford just to get to A-Gone's bat. But it was not enough to catch the Giants in the NL West, as San Francisco's acquisition of Marco Scutaro from the struggling Rockies paid off in a huge way. Suddenly in the thick of a postseason chase, the veteran infielder stepped up his game. He hit .362 over the remainder of the season with the Giants and earned MVP honors for his NLCS performance.

In the AL West, Texas found itself in need of starters. With Neftali Feliz out for the season after Tommy John surgery and Roy Oswalt dealing with a back injury, the team picked up starter Ryan Dempster from the Cubs. They completed their battery by bringing in catcher Geovany Soto from Chicago, as well. "I think being in contention gives you that second wind," said Soto, who ended his first month playing in Arlington on an 11-game hot streak during which he batted .325. "You always give 100 percent wherever you are, but coming here — to a different league, a different division — it's kind of like getting called up all over again."

WINS, ULTIMATELY, ARE what count. The 2011 Wild Cards, Tampa Bay and St. Louis, were determined on that crazy, final day of the regular season, when all that was supposed to happen was turned upside down. The Rays took the Wild Card at 91-71, the Cardinals at 90-72. The next-place finishers in each league, the Red Sox and Braves, had 90 and 89 wins, respectively. The threshold to get into the AL playoffs was higher in 2012, as the Rangers and Orioles won the two spots with 93 wins each. But in the NL, the Cardinals earned a Wild Card berth for the second year in a row despite ending the season six games behind the Braves. After making quick work of Atlanta in the one-game Wild Card elimination, the Redbirds, whose season would have already been over in previous years, nearly upset the division-winning Giants in the NLCS.

As 2012 showed, with many key teams finishing the year miles away from where they started, MLB's new postseason and future deadline deals promise to be wilder than ever. ◆

MINOR LEAGUE
RESULTS

AAA FRESNO GRIZZLIES (74-70)

3rd in PCL Pacific South Division

AA RICHMOND FLYING SQUIRRELS (70-71)

4th in Eastern League Western Division

HIGH-A SAN JOSE GIANTS (75-65)

1st in California League North Division

A AUGUSTA GREENJACKETS (69-70)

5th in South Atlantic League Southern Division

MAJOR LEAGUE BASEBALL

Executive Vice President, Business   TIMOTHY J. BROSNAN

MAJOR LEAGUE BASEBALL PROPERTIES

Senior Vice President,
Consumer Products   HOWARD SMITH
Vice President, Publishing   DONALD S. HINTZE
Editorial Director   MIKE McCORMICK
Publications Art Director   FAITH M. RITTENBERG
Senior Production Manager   CLAIRE WALSH
Account Executive, Publishing   CHRIS RODDAY
Senior Publishing Coordinator   JAKE SCHWARTZSTEIN
Associate Art Director   MARK CALIMBAS
Associate Editor   ALLISON DUFFY
Project Assistant Editors   HANNAH KEYSER
BRIAN KOTLOFF
Editorial Interns   JORDAN RABINOWITZ
GERALD SCHIFMAN

MAJOR LEAGUE BASEBALL PHOTOS

Manager   JESSICA FOSTER
Photo Editor   JIM McKENNA
Intern   JOSH HAUNSCHILD

Project Contributing Photographers   BRAD MANGIN
RON VESELY

THE McCLELLAND & STEWART/FENN TEAM
JORDAN FENN
LINDA PRUESSEN
MICHAEL MELGAARD
JAMES YOUNG, RUTA LIORMONAS
JANINE LAPORTE

PHOTO CREDITS

Ron Vesely/MLB Photos: Cover (celebration, Posey, Zito); 4 (Romo); 6; 8 (Tigers, Perry); 9 (Phillips); 10 (fans); 11 (3); 12 (Sandoval); 54 (Zito); 58–59; 60; 62 (2); 65 (Laird); 67; 68; 70–71; 72; 73; 75 (3); 78–79 (Romo); 80; 93; 94; 108; 132 (Fielder); 140 (All-Star Game, Fielder); 150 (Uribe)

Brad Mangin/MLB Photos: Cover (Sandoval); 4–5; 8 (jersey); 9 (bats, cage); 10 (kid, Pence); 12 (Posey, Theriot); 14–15 (3); 52; 53; 54 (Verlander); 55 (3); 56; 57; 64–65; 66; 69; 74; 76 (2); 79 (Pence & Theriot, Posey); 88; 91; 97; 98–99; 103 (2); 104; 105; 106; 107; 109; 110; 111 (2); 113; 114 (2); 117; 118; 119 (2); 121; 122; 123; 126; 127; 128; 130; 131; 135; 137; 143; 144 (Athletics); 145; 157; 158

Jed Jacobsohn/MLB Photos: 4 (Posey); 20; 21; 22; 23

Ezra Shaw/Getty Images: 4 (Pence); 33 (2); 49; 51 (Romo)

Duane Burleson/MLB Photos: 13; 77

Jonathan Daniel/Getty Images: 24; 30; 31

John Grieshop/MLB Photos: 25; 26 (2); 27; 132 (Cabrera); 146 (Cabrera)

Andy Lyons/Getty Images: 28; 29

Thearon W. Henderson/Getty Images: 32; 34; 36; 37 (Carpenter)

Christian Petersen/Getty Images: 35; 37 (Vogelsong); 46; 47; 48; 51 (locker room); 98 (McCovey Cove); 148; 154

Elsa/Getty Images: 38; 39 (Carpenter); 43; 44–45 (Zito); 87

Kevin C. Cox/Getty Images: 39 (tarp); 40; 41; 44 (Zito)

Dilip Vishwanat/Getty Images: 42

David J. Phillip/Pool/Getty Images: 50

Rob Leiter/MLB Photos: 61; 63

Library of Congress: 82

National Baseball Hall of Fame: 83; 84 (2); 85

Rob Tringali/MLB Photos: 102; 112 (Huff); 120; 124; 125; 141

Missy Mikulecky/San Francisco Giants: 112 (Kontos); 116; 139

Andy Kuno/San Francisco Giants: 115

Doug Pensinger/Getty Images: 129

Cincinnati Reds: 132 (Votto); 136

Mike Stobe/Getty Images: 132 (Dickey); 138

Jason O. Watson/Getty Images: 133

Jon SooHoo/Los Angeles Dodgers: 134 (Kemp)

Winslow Townson/MLB Photos: 134 (Red Sox)

Mike Ehrmann/Getty Images: 136 (Stanton)

Mitchell Layton/Washington Nationals: 136; 144 (Nationals)

Jordan Megenhardt/Arizona Diamondbacks: 138 (Hill)

Scott Cunningham/Getty Images: 138 (Beltran)

Justin K. Aller/Getty Images: 140 (Pirates)

Al Bello/Getty Images: 142 (Jeter)

Ed Zurga/Getty Images: 142 (Dunn); 146

Boston Red Sox: 146 (Yaz)

Louis Requena/MLB Photos: 146 (Robinson)

Rich Pilling/MLB Photos: 150 (Cain); 151; 152 (Kinsler)

Justin Sullivan/Getty Images: 152 (parade); 153

Pittsburgh Pirates: 156